FIRST COMMANDMENT REVISITED

The Human Imperative

FIRST COMMANDMENT REVISITED

The Human Imperative

DAM-UYEN DINH TRAN

http://www.transinformation.com
Blaine, Minnesota
U.S.A.

Dam-Uyen Tran is available for interviews and panel discussions. Please contact the publisher below, or e-mail the author at dudtran@transinformation.com.

Quantity discounts for educational, religious, and military organizations are available. Please contact the publisher immediately.

Thank you.

http://www.transinformation.com/
1512—125th Avenue NE
PMB 107
Blaine, Minnesota
U.S.A.
Mpls/St. Paul: 1 (612) 767-2270
Toll Free: 1 (877) 319-5580
tif@transinformation.com

CONTRIBUTORS

Cover Art	Hanh Vo
Cover Design	Dam-Uyen Tran
Drawings	Hanh Vo
Illustrations	Dam-Uyen Tran
Content Editor	Kay Vang
Technical Editor	Paul Konrad
Copy Editor	Christina Nebel
Inspirational Source	All people of the human race

DEDICATION

I dedicate this book and all desirable results it brings to my forgiving wife and patient children.

I count on *FIRST COMMANDMENT REVISITED: The Human Imperative* and other books like it to change the world we live in— especially for our children and future generations.

***

IMPORTANT NOTICE

The author, Dam-Uyen D. Tran, made every effort where applicable to be indiscriminate— socially, racially, religiously, and politically. In addition, the author and his publisher, TransInFormation, practice gender fairness in all practical areas— in thoughts, language, and in print.

Furthermore, the author does not represent any social, racial, political, religious, or military group.

This book, *FIRST COMMANDMENT REVISITED: The Human Imperative*, contains explicit views and opinions solely of the author, who makes no guarantee in any degree including but not limited to validity, correctness, appropriateness, or practicality— when taken in, as well as out of, context.

Moreover, inferences, dates, statistics, and quotations belong to their respective original sources. No guarantee is made regarding the accuracy of quotations from these and other sources.

The author and his publisher shall not be held liable for any use and subsequent results derived directly or indirectly from interpretations of this book, or other books mentioned herein.

Please consult your religious leaders, political representatives, social workers, doctors, legal advisors, family counselors, etc. before applying or engaging methods outlined herein, or derived wherefrom.

This book is strictly for a mature audience.

***

TABLE OF CONTENTS

***

PREFACE

The goal of this book
is to change
the
world.

If we do not change our direction,
we are likely to end up where we are headed.
— Ancient Chinese Proverb

THE MOTIVATION

It is quite clear today that evolutionary scholars, theologians, and common people alike have yet to offer practical answers to the apparent escalating evil around the world.

This book shows that people can adopt ways of life that will reflect true human capacities. It unveils subtle hypocrisies undermining people's established values, beliefs, and purpose, genuinely offering practical answers everyone can realistically apply.

To achieve new understanding, we must be willing to read messages without imposing our successes and failures onto them. To arrive at new solutions, we must open ourselves to possibilities, to which our finite experience may not relate.

From our experience, some people equate so-called facts with truths. As vast information in the world conditions us to be selective, "Is it a fact?" has become the mechanism we use to make our selections. Casually, we dismiss everything else as fiction or opinions, and neglect to ask ourselves some important questions:

Can such facts merely weather the test of time, or can they survive the consistency test? Are such facts supported by so-called evidence, or are they self-evident? Do they obscure realities, or do they illuminate to the truth?

"Is it a fact?" satisfies our credibility requirement, but falls short of answering another important question: Is credibility a measure of agreeability, popularity, or instancy? Are we more concerned with whether it agrees with what we want to hear, inducts us into a larger crowd, or promise us some "quick fix"?

Why is credibility not a measure of adherence to the truth?

Various groups and cultures spend money on big authors and endorse issues with big poll numbers. We believe in certain propaganda because we can recognize the associations that they make. All of that, perhaps until now, has been the basis for what people call "credibility."

In this book, credibility means the relative degree to which a subject or claim is consistent in life.

To transcend basic understanding is to expect truth and integrity, which surpass facts and credibility. To achieve new understanding, we must appreciate ideas expressed in manners unlike before. We must not assume that words only have traditional meanings whether in writing, speech, or thought.

This is only possible by acknowledging that while words have meanings in themselves, as you and I do independently, each must suspend individual significance and work together at new heights.

However, we must be careful not to take it too far. Like reading a book about illnesses, we may recognize familiar symptoms and associate them to ourselves. While some people reassure themselves, "There's nothing wrong with me," others may schedule appointments to check out the illnesses they believe they've had all along.

You will also find symptoms in this book you think point to you; like the book about illnesses, this one does not attack you personally.

This book is not another interpretation of the Bible, the Torah, the Koran, or other religious writings. With a few exceptions, it doesn't call on, borrow from, or support other books. This is a life-saving exercise of the human thinking machine, to prepare our minds as the tools of the future.

Until you are sure of what you read, do not go further and risk a misunderstanding, albeit insignificant. You will be expected to think on your own, but recognize the difference between independent thinking and imposing your own meanings to what's being expressed.

Having said that, I make no argument about whether your God or my God is the one Creator, as I'm perfectly comfortable referring to yours instead of mine. This comfort comes from the fact that there must be one and only one Almighty God. Why? It's precisely because if your God is almighty—then mine is necessarily "almighty" minus one... or two, or more.

It follows that there must be one and only one Throne. As long as I make it to the foot of the one Throne, I am perfectly content if the God is yours. I must not climb a stool and think I have found the great kingdom.

If each religious group takes comfort in worshipping only one God, then humankind, as the larger group— must also have one God.

I cannot teach anybody anything,
I can only make them think.
— Socrates

The Beginning

THE BEGINNING

When our world first came into existence some un-told millenniums ago, life began from the void and the void was overtaken. Because human history does not recall witnessing the incredible formation, we were not there in all probability. Realistically, it could have been billions of ages ago; we cannot tell for sure.

Eventually, a voice cried out in the vast kingdom that would become populated with humankind. There were animals and, soon, we noticed other living and non-living life forms around us. The place was no longer quiet.

It was gradually evident that the world would tend toward disorder, corruption, and inevitable destruction, if a governor were not promptly put in place. No need for an election yet though, as the Maker was still eager to tend to the details.

You know, the yolk of Life is carried and delivered by the bearer, or woman, as we have seen consistently. We may insist that God is more than both man and woman, but certainly not only man. While the use of human pronouns cannot change the nature of Almighty God, we need to be consistent so we can prevail.

In the spirit of correctness and consistency, we will no longer refer to God as Father, Him, His, or Himself. Instead, we begin a new allegiance to *Parents, Them, Their,* or *Them-*

selves, respectively. While this usage can be cumbersome, we must not over-simplify God for our convenience. I am not suggesting a new tradition of polytheism, but I insist we recognize that God is irrefutably multi-faceted and altogether complete. As we err, we must err on the plural side.

Maintaining order or establishing the rule of law became an important universal investment. God's terms hence followed and were called commandments. All of God's creations did fear *Them*, thus over untold months and years that followed, *Their* creations obediently observe the rules of law. Consequently, it became revered as keeper of harmony and guarantor of lasting order. As life became increasingly permanent, it also appeared that those terms were becoming the lasting governor for humankind.

Obedience to the governor evolved into life itself for people. Observing obedience became their occupation and, ironically, persecution. Nonetheless, there was a rhythm to life and ensuing death, where the human mechanics found a way to hold back the judgment on the human race thus far.

Time gradually proved that obedience alone raised questions and instilled doubts as to whether there was a real penalty. With so many questions and so little knowledge, where could people even begin? Questions were boiling within our individual selves as well as among each other, in our effort to survive. Subsequently, people began to wonder, "Why are we here?"

Individuals from Judeo-Christian traditions might argue that people haven't been obedient since the first humans committed the "original sin." That was when Adam and Eve ate the forbidden fruit. We still talk about education even though we might not be educated. Obedience, then, is something we must work on and talk about, even though we're not completely obedient.

Before answers could be secured, more looming questions threatened the earlier established order. "Who are you anyway?" for example, and the basic question, "Who am I?"

Soon, people staked out territories and erected walls to keep out those they feared or did not recognize. They didn't build these walls exclusively with bricks, stones, or wood; they also built these walls with selfishness, disrespect, and self-righteousness. The territorial walls became divisions within our own kind, and people became accustomed to guarding boundaries. Warriors drew battle lines, fighters took opposite corners of the court, and God suddenly appeared to take sides.

Like two armies, two boxers pray for a safe victory—knowing fully that only one will thank God at the end.

People as individuals also divided, as they could no longer see their whole beings. Whether we ever could see our whole beings before, we had become most visibly physical, mental, emotional, psychological, and spiritual beings. It's as if we were each, in ourselves, one individual but no longer singular— like God in a way.

It appeared the sitting "governor" became inadequate.

The human progression seemed irreversible beginning with our territorial acts, the political God, the dividing selves, and the deficient governor. God, too, was changing. They were in the beginning *Parents*, but now *They* were emerging as God only of the spiritual selves, while people sought out additional masters they saw fit to lead the other selves within them.

New allegiances were formed with psychologists for our psychological selves, doctors for our physical health, and money and goods for our material selves. Additionally, we held elections for rulers, kings, and presidents.

We eventually learned about ourselves through psychologists, looked for healing from physicians, and measured our success with wealth; answered to royalties, all the while praying to God.

Allegiance became perpetual human-imposed servitude.

During the course of preservation and maintenance, people began to lose sight of the basic and once passionate questions in their will to survive. As humanity continued to progress, these questions loomed ever larger until we were forced to look away for the most part. The rule of law, once established, was overshadowed increasingly by political, social, and economical regimes, which can only try to understand the new meta-human mechanics. These are no longer just humans but, more precisely, physical, mental, and spiritual selves.

The earlier rhythm of order is now synchronized with a foreign impulse to withdraw interest from the apparent peace before.

"I don't know that there was ever peace," a Sunday school teacher argued. Sure, you must see that there was peace, absolutely, until humankind introduced war— or sinned, if you prefer. Peace clearly permeated all realms well before humankinds' beginning, prescribed by the very nature of Almighty God.

Moreover, we have even detached ourselves from humanity to lessen the burden of association we can't seem to shoulder anymore. While we live out our lives "just making ends meet," questions remain and doubts infest the "selves" in you and me.

Can we get our *selves* together, assemble, and pledge for one last time— to remain?

Can we prevail?

Do we know?

Humankind has not woven the web of life.
We are but one thread within it.
Whatever we do to the web, we do to ourselves.
All things are bound together.
All things connect.
— Chief Seattle

The Flat Mind

THE FLAT MIND

People once believed that earth was the center of the universe, the focus of all life forms and energy. The sun and the moon were rising and setting in definite motions, as if God had assigned them to accompany us day and night perpetually. The power to produce life and the energy to sustain it all seemed to originate from where we stood.

We eventually found this was not true.

Human-centered notions of life had to be changed, and a system of new applications gradually replaced the earlier establishment, or culture and order of life. Science and astronomy, in particular, had to be re-calculated, re-established, and re-articulated. Education was modified to reflect the new center of the universe— which was to be somewhere else.

People also believed the earth was flat, and there was a point beyond which we would fall off or could possibly crawl onto the other side. They had persuasive supporting evidence, so conclusions offered by the learned people of the day must have been correct.

In time, we discovered how naïve that belief was, too. Another standing "fact" was revoked. Elaborate systems of life, education, and culture required changing. Beliefs and establishments would be altered dramatically. As some simplistic examples, maps were redrawn, and human travel was charted all over again.

These misconceptions came from people's dependency on visual cues. Throughout history, we have come to accept that "seeing is believing." While relying on our extraordinary vision, we can disregard other perceptive faculties. We must wonder whether the power is in the testimony, or in our eyes.

Let me explain. Powerful testimony, or evidence, might exist for our sense of intuition, or our understanding of right and wrong. Granted, many of us may have written intuition off as fictional. The perceptive power of our eyes can mislead us, and cause us to misdirect and become dependent. For example, a powerful telescope distinctly reveals the subjects it's pointing at, but it also denies us the broader scope outside of its relatively diminutive field of view.

Our perceptive apparatus including the eyes, ears, nose, and nerves do not provide the proofs— but they can deny us countless evidence.

Because we now realize the world isn't flat, we resort to accepting the spherical reality. Nonetheless, we are still only good at drawing two-dimensional pictures or visualizing simple two-dimensional ideas. While we technically accepted the three-dimensional world, we have not actively grown in it, nor progressed in using it. While we might accept a different point as the focus of the universe, our thoughts and actions are still self-centered.

Our minds have remained flat in other ways. We still think that we are the reason for Life, as we have historically disregarded other living things and exploited natural wonders. Many people still perceive that wrongs are committed against us or to harm us, while there might be no malice at all. Many of us are still convinced that the universe and everything in it are only for us to use, consume, and define.

America didn't exist until a group of people "found it." No one asked for its name or wondered about its owner. It's as if our discovery is actually grander than the creation itself. It's as if something was real because humans found it.

Additionally, most of us believe extraterrestrials look like us. We paint God with a face we recognize. We even think ghosts have hands, feet, and a face as we do. People don't explicitly choose to depict these figures like this; they simply cannot conceive things differently, because of the limited extent to which they use their minds.

Should we stop sketching if we don't have the picture? Not at all. Allow your imagination the freedom to visualize the images that we have and have not seen. However, do not think that a substitute can ever become the real thing, merely because we believe it for a long time— no more than an opinion becoming truth because the majority honors it.

Realizing at some level that our minds are constrained, people fascinate themselves with those "who can think outside the box," because we know for the most part we can't. Here is a good "proof" that most of us cannot think beyond our usual borders: arrange nine dots into a perfect square (i.e. three rows of three dots), then draw four straight lines without lifting the pen, such that each dot is crossed at least once.

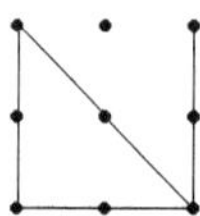

Incorrect

I don't know about your first tries, but it was not obvious to me until the answer was revealed. This example isn't elaborate, but it shows that we can get quite boxed up mentally.

Experience and expectation can dull another perceptive faculty, known as common sense. Common sense is, essentially, the ability to make sound judgment beyond our combined experience and expectations. The more people experience or know, ironically, the more rigid they tend to become. They can react more, and permit fewer possibilities.

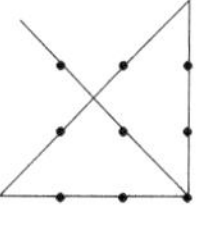

Correct

Experience and expectation seamlessly govern our thoughts, shape our lives and, in effect, take away our freedom to think creatively without limitation. They also impose heavily on our understanding of dimensions such as time, space, and other possibilities.

Consider spatial navigation, for example. People can negotiate fairly well, as long as they remain within "line of sight." Beyond that, humans require various instruments to get around. Recall how you or your friends dreaded elementary geometry or trigonometry, because it was difficult to imagine space.

People are much worse when it comes to temporal accountability. What happened 24 hours ago is as much your guess as it is mine, and usually requires us to recount where we were, what we were doing, and what else might have been around us. How well we account for time depends on our recollection of the previously mentioned dimension— or space.

Granted, we no longer believe in a two-dimensional flat world, we still lack the maturity to manage a three, four, or five-dimension reality. Additionally, from our experience and expectation, there's a limitation as to what we would accept as real or plausible. This further amplifies our cognitive handicap. Perhaps that's why people are intense about defending what they can grasp.

In much the same way, many of us have difficulties with the spiritual dimension. We cannot perceive this dimension as readily as the spatial dimension using our eyes, or the temporal dimension using a clock. As a result, spirituality has been relatively arbitrary, when compared to most other aspects of our lives. Notice that we can be extremely perceptive, pensive, and responsive whether a dimension is concrete and tangible, or abstract and intangible.

We can measure time, use it as a tool, live and die in it. People can negotiate and "buy time," draw contracts and cast judgment in time. While not tangible, time is a dimension most people believe in, agree on, and build lives around. On the other hand, religion or a system of values, beliefs, and spiritual practices, presents more challenges with much less consensus. For example, we can agree on a time or a place, but— "Everyone is entitled to their own religious beliefs."

This is because the quest for survival lured us into believing that customary dimensions are more critical and profitable. Quietly some people admit that religion does not deliver like the post office, and does not pay like a good job. At the least, it's clearly hard to confirm, and its effects on our lives are even less verifiable or quantifiable.

We visit doctors for physical remedies, psychologists for psychological healings, and politicians for societal solutions, and can see real effects relatively quickly. One election and we can change political opinions. Thirty minutes with a psychologist and we can be more motivated. Doctors may have little good news to report, but we typically have the results fairly soon. With God, it's more imprecise.

All this makes it difficult to enforce religion or deter and punish offenders. In fact, our political or social associations, or even economical ones, carry more enforcement power than our religious positions. The taxman solicits more compliance than any religious advocate could, at least in this day and age. Many people swear not to kill, but will engage in wars if they can identify an enemy.

Religion has taken a back seat in life to either resign or function in a backup role. We will buy a newer car if the old one becomes a problem, fix the roof right away if it leaks, and schedule a vacation just as soon as we have time. Regrettably, we tend to make religion a project for a rainy day.

You probably know of people who live in strict accordance to their faith every single day, but you should understand that I am talking about a bigger picture. I am not saying that religious thoughts and practices are non-existent. I do insist, however, that other "thoughts" and "practices" do largely take precedence.

Where is the proof? Simply look at people. Have we really advanced spiritually? If everyone in the "bigger picture" truly lived in religious harmony, we wouldn't leave our spirituality behind.

Some people would be correct for pointing out that things in life, including the religious "dimension," are not always black and white, or right and wrong. Perhaps that's true, but we must realize that human's consciousness and cognitive capacity may be questionable, while our obligation to God is not. It shouldn't be difficult to recognize what we will accept arbitrarily and what we will accept only near absolutely.

I do trust that you understand your spiritual connection and know your responsibility. Otherwise, life as you know it is final with you.

We must apply our spiritual capacities as we do other capacities. We must exercise our spiritual perception as we apply other perceptions everyday.

Let's for the moment assume that you and I are spiritual people with fears, desires, and strengths, who are certain that the circle of life goes beyond the relentless reiterations of expectations, temptations, and daily bread. We believe there is a post-physical life or some sort of continuance, where "Life" continues with a different breadth. Something, we insist, must elevate us from other life forms.

Let's allow that we may believe, individually, in our God.

I elect not to discuss creationism or evolution here because, as you will see, it all becomes less and less important as to when in time we were created or where in life we may have changed.

When we gain true respect for roses, it's suddenly insignificant what sizes or colors they grow, or the sequence their petals bloom, wouldn't you agree? We instinctively absorb all of their fragrance and embrace their unequivocal beauty. Creationism, evolution, and other theories also drop out of focus when we become re-oriented. We then come to understand why we tend to fixate on irrelevance, and obscure our yearning for truths.

We can only construct with the tools we possess, and work with the apparatus we are given. If we cut the handle of our hoe too short, we will lose leverage. If we forge too small a hammer, we take away the power. If we close our perceptive abilities too soon, we will miss the vision.

What fallacies will be discovered tomorrow in what we hold to be so true today?

In this book, we will address issues that have been plaguing humankind for as long as generations have lived. We will tackle issues as you have never experienced before, and we will rebuild them with tools that we've left idle since the beginning.

We begin at *The Origin*, because all human thoughts, actions, notions, and beliefs are rooted in "the origin." Our expectation, perception, and comprehension of our origin govern what we expect of ourselves, how we perceive truth, and to what level we understand Life.

In *The Monkey*, we'll see how misconceptions can keep us in illusions for thousands of years. Inferiority then works its ways seamlessly into our lives and holds us firmly until death. *The Inferiority* reminds us that we must live productive and superior lives, so with confidence we can prosper on our permanent journey— rather than wait out despairingly for the end. We will find in *The Prophets* that we cannot choose an end for which to live, because it is in our living that an end is defined.

For instance, consider heaven as an "end." *The Heaven* shows us that much of what humans do evolves around this end, and what humans become is less deserving of the same end. To make this seemingly impossible correction is to look closely at our doctrines. *The Dogma* reveals that religious institutions are not capable of delivering humankind to Almighty God. These institutions condition us to live life tentatively, without fulfillment, as exemplified by *The Paper Plate*.

The Human Struggle ensues, consequently, because religions cannot deliver obscure promises. Pain and tribulation will grip us until we can affirm the vision of God in our minds in *The Image*. *The Essence* shows us who we are, and offer ways to attain self-intimacy. Self-imaging is critical, if we endeavor to know Life, and avoid succumbing to hope. *The Hope* dispells the age-old power humans assign to the fleeting notion, and reveals how hope feeds on human anguish. We will find ways to replace hope with "knowing."

The Resolution removes usesless pretenses, harmful doubts, and empty promises. Then we'll assemble all that we discover, and elevate humanity to its heights. To ensure we achieve our goal this time, *The Devil* explains how to eliminate the "prince of darkness" and his interference, with confidence.

The Final Victory will deliver us from physical and spiritual imprisonment.

The Messiah, of course, still waits for us at the end.

All that we are is the result of what we have thought.
— The Buddha

The Origin

THE ORIGIN

"If we cut the handle of our hoe too short, we will lose leverage. If we forge too small a hammer, we take away the power. If we close our perceptive abilities too soon, we will miss the vision."
— The Flat Mind

An interesting question to ponder, as we proceed, is whether the origin and the destination are the same place. Some people may assert that these are neither physical places nor anything we can conceive in our minds.

I would suggest that the origin and destination are a harmonious union of all possible realities. The origin is where all life commences, while the destination is where all life returns. The operative word here is "all." The place, time, or element that contains all possibilities must necessarily exist only once. Look at it this way: If there are two baskets of eggs, neither one contains all of the eggs.

If the origin contains all possibilities, as does the destination— they must be the same "place."

We should discover our meaningful origin, so we can comprehend the direction, and purpose, of Life.

Our entire life and, more specifically, the decisions we make depend strictly on our understanding of the origin, along with our perception of the destination. Individual successes and the propagation of the human species hinges directly on this fundamental starting point.

What is the origin of human life?

Many people believe life originated from astronomical events, in which simple life forms evolved into complex genuses. This approach or perspective doesn't examine authorship; instead it assumes ownership. This approach doesn't recognize that there might be a mastermind, while it offers explanations and justifications as if it were.

One answer is that human life began deliberately, predicating that, fundamentally, we owe our originality to the Creator. All that we become and produce throughout our lives may ultimately fulfill the Creator's agenda.

When we accept that the *place*, which contains all possibilities, exists only once, we may realize that there is little need to reconstruct historical contexts and ambiguous facts. Because the destination and origin are the same, it is more productive to research and invest in the future, rather than philosophical pasts.

Let's re-orient our minds to the life, direction, and promise before us.

We must let go of the evolution-versus-creationism contention, for they address entirely different questions. Plausible or not, evolution can only explain how life changes or evolves, as no life form remains unchanged.

God expects people to progress— from spiritual vagrants to *destination seekers*, from self-centered sinners to selfless humanity. Let's agree to change from a questionable species to unquestionable descendants of God, by carrying ourselves to *The Final Victory*.

Knowing is not enough; we must Apply.
Willing is not enough; we must Do.
— Goethe

The Monkey

THE MONKEY

"We must let go of the evolution-versus-creationism contention, for they address entirely different questions. Plausible or not, evolution can only explain how life changes or evolves, as no life form remains unchanged."

— *The Origin*

One premise of evolution suggests that humans evolved from primates. Many people are uncomfortable being *related* to primates, and created in God's image at the same time. However distasteful this theory may be, we gamble the awesome risk of also denying the Author by rejecting it as a possibility.

What injuries could this cause to the relationship we try to foster with God, the sole Author of the entire universe?

As a stretching exercise of our perception, let's consider the apes for a moment. They obviously lack some human intelligence, and the visual beauty many people would wish for themselves; nonetheless, we can agree that they do have primate intelligence and striking beauty of their own. We must admit that we might not have thought about the possibility that humans aren't the intended species, despite superfluous appearances.

Recall from *The Flat Mind* that perception doesn't precipitate truth. While walking completely erect, perhaps we are the ones to have squandered and strayed. Although technologically complex, humans might be the ones who confuse the equation of Life.

How dare I suppose such an idea?

Think intrinsically why most of us are so quick to reject such a thought. Priding ourselves for learning from our mistakes, what have we learned from the flat earth or the anthropocentric universe?

Since the concept of an earth-centered universe was proven incorrect, people should have emerged with broadened viewpoints. By learning from our mistakes, we should become more discriminating, yet more tolerant over the millennia.

Is it possible that apes have left us behind in the spiritual evolution?

Maybe the primates have found a way to commune with the Creator, no longer rehearsing repetitious rituals that many people embrace as religious faith. Let's not judge other species' fitness to be children of God, because there is progress we must be making as well.

As prescribed by many religions, people have been practicing obedience, repentance, and redemption faithfully. Lately, though, it's been difficult to distinguish between human tradition and true communion with God.

For example, people don't walk through life claiming or self-reassuring who their parents are. We don't do that because there has been no dispute. If you tell me that someone is your mother or father, I won't argue with you. No one has ever challenged us as to who our parents are, even though some people may have unique family circumstances. We only need to introduce and claim our parents once, be they adoptive or biological.

Consequently, who is disputing about the *Parents* in your life?

Let us work toward a day when we can look into one another's eyes and appreciate, "Naturally, I know who your *Parents* are."

Many people believe they do certain rituals out of respect for God. I must ask: What is the theory behind thousands and thousands of years of mourning? More specifically, do any spiritual people worship a dead god, ironically, for a life after? Of course not, but human's practices would indicate otherwise.

Some people practice religion, or rituals, every year. Some people do it every week and others do it every day. Many religions teach that practicing certain rituals once a day is not enough, as if God suffers from the same "remembering" disorder that afflicts many humans.

Why must we make a habit out of our relationship with God?

Are we still trying to buy into the whole god notion?

After all, we are not this elaborate and mechanical in our relationship with our human parents, although they are extremely important to us, too.

Invariably, your God has ascended in one medium or another by conquering death— or never died. Humans' death rituals suggest that people haven't grieved enough. Perhaps people have buried frustrations in that their God could die.

"Who's mourning?" a respected Lutheran argues. "We worship a risen Lord, and there is joy and peace in that." I know Christians recognize what Lent and Easter are all about.

Perhaps mourning is a poor choice of words, but we could really coin the 40 days of fasting and penitence anything we wish.

We would never conduct funerals years after years for our living mother, father, or friend. The God that you and I worship, different or the same, is alive. Furthermore, we shall see together, *They* never died.

Mourning, as modern doctors would say, is healing for the living. Well then, we must stop scarring and wounding ourselves over and over, if we're serious about a remedy. That's precisely what we will explore in *The Human Struggle*.

Aside from the death event, we rehearse other rituals as well. One such rehearsal is giving praises. Religions across the world hum, chant, and sing praises to God. This practice can range from murmurs, to choruses, to bellows depending on when and where it is.

Are people really getting their gratitude to God?

There is a conductor standing before the choir. There is a book of prayers in worshipers' hands— and somehow everyone agree unanimously to be thankful inside? To an impartial eye, it looks like the choir pulls off another recital, while the congregation once again passes the same lip service.

Sadly, some people may have reasons to hold the praises, as they don't think that God has been doing such a good job during the past few thousand years. Some of us have been praying in suffering for decades, and are now growing disheartened about our own loyalty— this whole idea of believing just a little more, and hanging on just a bit longer.

We still see injustice inflicting those we cannot help. Sons and daughters still practice shooting to kill. Repeat offenders still stalk unsuspecting victims. Somewhere, hearts still haven't mended. Additionally, many people have difficulties rationalizing the horrible faultless accidents and natural disasters that happen regularly.

Nevertheless, people circulate books of praises as if they are most gracious, regardless of unrelenting circumstances.

Not true, some people may say. We count our blessings. We look on the bright side. This eventually gets difficult for even the best of us, when we become the victims of assaults, departing loved ones, or no-fault accidents.

Sometimes, it seems we really can't count on God when it has to matter. During times of personal sorrow, societal depression, or national havoc, we are simply unable to do much about it— at least, not the vast majority of us.

Don't get me wrong. I'm not disgruntled at God as my "tone of voice" might suggest here. I am disappointed, however, that people don't have the decency to "get on the level" with God. I'm not referring to getting resentments out in the open with a prejudiced neighbor, or getting on the same page with a presumptuous colleague. I'm referring to having an honest relationship with God; a consistent, mature relationship with our *Parents*.

Even though it appears that God only helps the victorious, God does not take sides. God does not cause the sufferings in Kosovo, Bosnia, or Vietnam, while it all looks mistakably like "part of God's plans." I will defend God in *The Human Struggle* but, for now, we need to question whether people are cognizant of their religious practices anymore. Do we know what we are expressing— or are we merely fulfilling conditioned obligations?

We must speak out to God rather than pretending to embrace books of praises or traditional creeds. From here on, we should find all that we utter to God from the bottom of our hearts. God doesn't need us to sugar coat our reactions to Life for *Them. They* need to know we are reacting, alive, and interested.

Remember that God is about love— not eulogy. Otherwise, we would have been created a very different species.

Additionally, we are not qualified to give God praises, however assuming we are. Instead, we should give *Them* subdued thanks and quiet affirmation that we are connected with *Them.*

Some people would contend that, beyond respect, such rehearsals serve to preserve tradition, to educate, and to remember.

First, tradition has nothing to do with these practices. One undeniable example of this fallacy is that we mettle aggressively with others' traditions rather than endear them. "The Smiths' have this crazy thing every year," and who cares about their inherent personal values. More gravely, "The Koreans… someone must stop them from doing that," because we don't find it acceptable, while we visit the Olympic games. Some people experience serious discomfort when traditions, in some way, do not suit their own.

Even for older cultures, merely practicing rituals serves as habitual veils, behind which are religious distrust, apathy, and callousness.

Try visiting your parents at the same time of the week, and see if that's respectful. Arrive with the same people, say some of the same things from the previous 52 weeks, and see if that's sensitive. To top if off, spend several weeks, or just a few days, every year having their funerals— never mind that they are alive!

The moral of this *Ridinghood* story is that the supposed visit is nothing more than a habit, a ritual, and it's probably a cumbersome one. Meanwhile, critical ingredients of consistent relationships are missing. These ingredients can be trust, empathy, and sensitivity, rather than "distrust, apathy, and callousness."

Be forewarned, your parents probably will not appreciate this.

Neither does God.

When following blindly, and accepting as *de facto* all that may trouble us, we miserably fail our responsibility to insist on the truth. The vast majority of us have questioned tradition's validity at times, yet many people continue to march to the empty pretenses of the masses.

Second, there are educational values in repetitious ceremonies, many people may defend, other than the "tradition" argument. These people insist that our children mimic our behaviors, and learn from the culture in which they grow. I agree with that observation. However, we must address the values of *mimicking* and *learning*, both of which have no inherent value in themselves. What is being mimicked and what is being learned is critical, because mimicking and learning can both be terrible events.

Third, there are people who argue that they repeat rituals or religious practices over and over to remember God.

I can only wonder why— such difficulty.

From the beginning of this chapter, I raised concerns about the repetitious death event, then touched on habitual prayers and praises. There is another practice of great repetition and abuse— the usage of religious texts.

Irrespective of religion, writers wrote testaments to their faith in God long ago. Without the journals of the early disciples, can we draw any testaments on our own? These testaments are the words of saints and disciples. Yes, but what's more significant is what you can testify on your own.

Yes, but "The writers are not just anyone. They are saints and holy people and God's chosen ones," you may say. Let me put it this way. Will you stand before God, one day, on your own conviction or on the conviction of saints and disciples from another time?

Foremost, we must recognize that however inspired or influenced, religious texts are written and translated by humans. We must accept that the gold trim around the Bible, the Torah, the Koran or any other such text is not a holy seal. These texts do not constitute the "Word of God," much less *Their* "Living Word."

Understand that I am not arguing whether God inspired the writers.

We don't need to go back, even a single day, in time to see how people summon and talk directly with their gods. Yes, they're inspired all right, but not only by God. It is critical that we discern what was inspired by God and what was stimulated by human practices.

Consider any group of aborigines, for instance. Sure, they are inspired, but I suspect they do not move you to the point of uncontested obedience.

Why do we insist that people are relatively subjective or partial today, but not thousands of years ago? More specifically, are humans flawless while inspired by God?

Call it the Bible of life. Call it the only authority in spiritual truth. Call it the key to God's kingdom, or a pass to Eden's backstage. Do not call it the "Living Word of God"— lest we violate the First Commandment, "Thou shall have no other gods."[1] This is precisely because if we call the words of proph-

---

[1] Exodus 20:3, *King James Bible*

ets or saints the "Living Word of God," we may be claiming that prophets and saints are gods. Of course, that is not what we mean, but that is exactly what we suggest.

We must also stop holding human-made articles above God, or as substitute for God, in seriousness or in light regardless of their content or context. We must realize that even if religious books are indeed holy articles, they must still be held subordinate to *Them*. We must not kiss or raise such articles in ceremonies lest we also violate the Second Commandment with presumed impunity. The Second Commandment forbids using human-made articles as images of God.[1]

Different religious faiths have their own order of commandments. What I'm trying to show here is that an elaborate faith is not necessarily a true one. We must ask, can it withstand the consistency test, or can it merely weather the "test of time"?

The human desire for containment cannot work with God. For instance, many people like to take a breathless landscape, and frame it in a five-by-seven photograph; some people like to take a sea-faring ship that tames the stormy blue depths, and seal it in a bottle. Can we contain the *Living Word* in a book?

This is not to criticize photography, bottling, or books, but we need to be keenly aware and sharply critical of processes we use, because we do not possess the origination privilege.

Understand— distinctly— we do not author God.

Beyond recognizing that however inspired, or influenced, religious texts are written by humankind, we must learn to use them appropriately. A critical part of this learning process involves adhering to the prime commandments prescribed by our religions, to ensure that we do not ineptly disqualify ourselves.

---

[1] Exodus 20:4-6, *King James Bibble*

If we cannot uphold the highest directives in any religion, there's little need to consider the remaining ones.

We should take these testaments about God, study them and understand them with the use of our available educational systems. Then, at a naturally appropriate age, we coach the students of Life through practical application, or internship, with the use of our cultures. Talk about God as we talk about football or soccer. Anticipate God in manners that we wait for holidays. Think of God not as a distant, esoteric, and frightening God— but as one who lives within us and beyond us. Know that God passes through us, stands beside us, and walks among us.

Integrate God into our lives.

Much like the multiplication tables, we all must painfully learn them. At the same time, we realize that they don't solve all problems. As we realize this limitation, we explore and expand into "internships" in daily life. From small multiplication tables, we can calculate how much things cost, figure out percentages, and expect change.

What's very clear is that we do not fixate on the multiplication tables themselves. If you recall, these tables form a relatively minute but fundamental basis in our ability to compute.

Multiplication does not compare to the study of God, people may argue; and they would be most right. I am not suggesting that we make any comparison. I trust you agree, however, that we better know how to multiply, if we endeavor to estimate the grandeur of God.

While the table helps us from basic survival to ingenious inventions, we do not envision it for anything more than what it is. In a way, it's the bible of the mathematical world— but we don't call it "living numbers."

From these multiplication tables and by them, we have moved on.

Like training wheels on a bicycle, which must be taken off before we can ride freely; religious texts must be surpassed, so that we can find our own intersection with God. Otherwise, we can't graduate to bigger bicycles, ride faster, see farther— and eventually go where God expects us to go.

It's time for self-definition and association with Life in and around us. It is time to recognize friends and enemies and the interdependence. It's time to make the "spiritual selves" the primary figures in our lives. It's time to make spirituality our dominant tradition.

Why not have a quiz show involving God? Broadcast "Spiritually Incorrect" on prime time television. Make Sunday a day of relationship: a day to invest in family and friends. By doing so, we can *profit* from a life devoted to God and not eulogy.

Before we can succeed in resolving human conflicts, we need to address how we really see ourselves as individuals, and as humans. Until we stand confidently, we can lose in match-ups against primates, other species, and circumstances in life.

We are what we repeatedly do.
— Aristotle

The Inferiority

THE INFERIORITY

Human inferiority doesn't come from discrimination or judgments from others. It comes from a fundamental and subtle cause— we don't know who we are. I'm sure you believe you know who you are. You are a man or a woman, a brother or a sister, a teacher and a student, a friend and a co-worker. You might be an out-going person, a reflective thinker, or a religious advocate. Nonetheless, we must know there is much more to us. Remember, we are endowments from God. Where we go with ourselves, though, is up to us.

A great number of us take ourselves to mediocrity, because we do not look to see our whole endowment. As suggested in *The Beginning*, "People as individuals also divided, as they could no longer see their whole being." This is further guaranteed by a notion we seamlessly allow— "I'm only human."

Suppose we call ourselves "entity," or something else without an inborn excuse. Try it next time for reasons that might bring you to uttering, "I'm only human." Say instead— I am "entity." Then take notice of how free you feel. If you don't feel the sensation, say again, "I am entity." Then say it aloud; then shout it time after time. If you cannot get it now, try it again for the next several millenniums, because we have dismissed ourselves at least that long.

We must see that limitations, while real, are not all that make up you and me. Suppose I am less than you in physical strength, mental quickness, or emotional endurance. Your family lineage may be one that is nationally recognized or even feared. I would have no misconception about how I compare with you, though admitting it might be difficult at first.

The power in being a human is that I am not obligated to feel, much less be, inferior to you. While you can overpower me, you can never own me, take away my endowment, or smear the One who authored me.

One automobile may be "inferior" to another because of a defect or a flaw. One photograph may be inferior to another in its fidelity to the real picture. Humans, though, reserve in themselves the power of choice to be different or better. It's as if they nurture inside a sleeping spirit of which no one can deprive them. It's a shine of "quality," if you will, that only their Creator can qualify. We must accept that only God can measure human quality.

While some individuals might be confident or superior, people, for the most part, cannot find the courage to stand alone. We need to understand that the conviction to stand alone precipitates an appreciation for the character itself and, unexpectedly, one new and united mass.

By upholding our endowment, we afford a new class of consensus. We result in a mass of one truth, instead of the earlier masses of individualism and popular notions. The mass of truth would consist of independent people looking in the same direction. The mass of "individualism" is a collective who "agree to disagree."

We may congregate to find strength for ourselves, or to contribute our strengths for all. The first congregation depletes, while the latter one fosters. The least we must expect from people is to know which congregation we each belong.

Whoever we are, however we enlist ourselves, let's agree that we must thoroughly understand the tools we use. Otherwise, the product or outcome becomes compromised. Look around and see how we use a piece of wood, a pencil, and a computer— and maybe one another. They all require that we invest genuinely in getting to know them.

Through the course of time, we learn better what to do with tools, but utterly lack in research and development of our higher selves. As if afraid to move on, we have been diligently working with mere models— the physical or corporal body-work of humanity. Meanwhile the ethereal aspects of our existence seem to have been ignored purposely.

Today, we have incredible technology with extraordinary capabilities to change the physical world with information, food, medicine, and bombs. Nevertheless, we struggle to improve ourselves in self-confidence, self-intimacy, and self-sufficiency. We can transport people to the moon, for example, but we have yet to advance our spirituality. We can repair human organs— but gamble that humanity refines itself.

The human history would corroborate our insecurities with many examples of war, slander, prejudice, and hate. Whether we produce our history with ignorance or with contempt, it shows our diffidence, or lack of self-confidence, as human beings.

To overcome diffidence is to first understand what it is. Various schools of thoughts theorize cause and effect differently, but let me suggest a direct approach to leveling this foundation. For social, economic, political, and other reasons diffidence exists, doubt is the common agent. This is to say that all types of people can be confident as long as they lack doubt. Most dictionaries define doubt as uncertainty, disbelief, distrust, suspicion, fear, and lack of conviction. We all can add a few more variances to what doubt ultimately is.

In any case, doubt is crippling.

Being as powerful and ominous as doubt is, we need to regard it as a disease, worthy of competition such as tuberculosis, AIDS, or any other human epidemic. While the concept of "doubtology" does not exist, people and our languages are more than capable of studying it, as long as we realize the urgency. We already agree with what it is, and recognize how it infects people; it's time we apply ourselves toward a cure.

Someone once said to me, "Doubt is good. Only fools are always sure of themselves and think they have all of the answers." How is this different from saying that we are sinners, and only dreamers think they can get to God? We clearly don't have all of the answers. It must be equally clear that we are working to find them.

I suspect doubt feeds us with chemicals to block the pains in our lives. Could doubt-induced anxieties produce neural agents for the brain that prepare us for pain? Doubt probably prepares us for both success and disappointment, or "At least, I'm mentally prepared." Without this buffer, we are mentally uncomfortable even though the trade-off is no more doubt—thus confidence. It makes us uneasy that in order to have no doubt, we have to neighbor willingly with pain.

Suppose we know that no more doubts means precisely no more pain? So rather than uncertainty, disbelief, distrust, suspicion, fear, and lack of conviction— we have certainty, coupled with the power of belief and trust. All the while, we would be without destructive suspicion and fear.

Are you genuinely ready to live without pain?

We can rid ourselves of our tentative stance amid Life only if we know of it. God purposefully endowed us with the brain and the power of choice. It is obvious that *They* didn't want us to be habitual, mechanical, or theatrical. Otherwise, a program would have done the job. Realizing that we have become complacent is only the first and necessary step to confidence.

Finally, to rid ourselves of doubt is to know!

Even though we might know only that we don't know, this knowing removes uncertainty and deprives "doubt" the opportunity to set off diffidence in us. Knowing that I don't know eliminates, "I think so," or "I'll do my best and see." We should know either affirmatively or negatively, but no more "I'm pretty sure."

There's no doubt when we truly know.

Try the new principle on this example: Do we *know* of another species that can doubt?

Besides ridding of doubts and replacing them with knowledge to further human advancement cooperatively, we have a responsibility to individually uphold ourselves. If you believe that we need to treat each other equally as neighbors and friends, givers and takers, you must also recognize your crucial and inexcusable responsibility; that is, to personally uphold yourself.

Inferiority is a state of self-neglect. Even while we treat others equitably and humanely, we continue to fall short of upholding ourselves. The tragic consequence of this self-neglect is that respect and equity fall short when not fueled by self-esteem.

We must recognize that while we expect others to treat us fairly and thoughtfully, we have yet the greater obligation— to see that the closest person to us does not fail. Not only is this expectation appropriate among humans, we must also apply the responsibility across all species. We may carry little obligation as a lesser order of life but, as the commanding genus, our responsibilities are clear.

On the other hand, there are people who believe humans have visibly evolved, progressed, and surpassed other species, especially when compared to our own ancient past. While we can incite or produce more in terms of results, not all has been commendable. The human family has been preoccupied with increasingly more high-tech machinery to beat time and its tragedies.

To sustain such engrossment, it casually replaces its own members with prosthetic marvels and surrogate imitations. Rather than developing ourselves, we expand technology. Instead of advancing humankind, we perfect machinery.

To educate, for example, we decimate forests in part to print books, produce papers, and build schools. From the same forests, we construct bigger, better, and safer houses only to leave a more barren habitat. Not only is this an immense expense paid by the very nature on which we depend, the devastation lies in the fact that the one hand seems clueless of what the other hand does.

The educator in us asks for books and the logger among us makes a living, so we happily oblige. The left hand holds the "dough," if you will, while the right hand holds the ax. We put a hammer in one hand, and our children in the other. Our babies grow up in bigger and stronger houses one day, only to find a thoughtlessly exhausted and expired future. However, the child would never know about it, because to her, it was always bare.

How do we expend other resources? What do we do about animal respect and protection? We need animals for food, labor, and other necessities of life, but there is no legitimate excuse for making spectacles and displays out of them. What is the great human idea with fur coats, sport hunting, the rodeo concept, or cock fighting?

I trust that you see how the pattern of human insecurity and doubt reduces us, and we, in turn, disrespect other resources and living things around us. Lacking esteem for our selves, we struggle to sustain respect for the rest of God's creations.

Consider that most living things have adaptations they evolve over time to help them better co-exist in their shared system. The operative word is "co-exist." They do not hunt a species to extinction to improve their own survival. They have not become conductors and engineers, scientists or even prophets. Nor have they devised and introduced into this coexistence the challenges and chaos that threaten the balance of all life. Today, many people still stand before a backdrop of primates, and tout humans' relative progress.

"Humans have a larger brain," let us remember. Let us also understand that the more pertinent question is— "Larger than whose?"

I insist that we have the larger capacity or, as we said earlier in this chapter, endowment. Sadly, we have provided ample evidence that this capacity has not been well developed. Yes, we have made great strides medically and technologically and more, but only reactively. We have been forced by the choices we make to live in different manners than our forefathers, as they did from their ancestors.

The threshold species we use to benchmark ourselves have seemingly been steadfast. This contrast, change relative to steadfastness, is somehow interpreted as human progress.

Ironically, it isn't hard to see how poorly we communicate, even today, compared to many other species such as dolphins, whales, and birds, to name a few. Dolphins, for example, evolved to best suit themselves, and became very skilled, proficient, and impressive as dolphins. This, they accomplish moreover without posing threats to the wild world kingdom, not even to humans, or forcing others to pay a serious price for their progress.

Every species that remains today does so by ingeniously changing itself, by using nature to the fullest extent yet somehow thoughtfully preserving its delicate alliance. Is it because we have "surpassed" other life forms that we don't have to be a member of this cooperative?

Changing or adapting people for life's sake as all other life forms do, would not be consistent with our egocentric pattern of adaptation. We have not become any better at being humans. We really have not set forth, in any perspective, even a small example of superiority. We progress down the line of time systematically, from inventing wheels to manufacturing spacecraft, from making stone arrowheads to building nuclear warheads— only to emerge farthest from humanity.

To remedy inferiority and disrespect, we must satisfy the knowledge criterion. *The Image* will show us how we can refine our "essence" and become intimate with ourselves, as other species have thrived in their own intimacy. Until then, we must accept that people have been perfecting impressive but superfluous hardware, if we're to recognize the extent of our diversion.

Realize, now, that our tangible and superficial proliferation thus far is unable to compensate for ruins in human lives.

To arrive at God, or to merely find enlightenment in our lives, we need to discover our "souls" and bridge them, if we endeavor to gap the distance between us and the Divine.

No one can make you feel inferior without your consent.
— Eleanor Roosevelt

The Prophets

THE PROPHETS

"I trust that you see how the pattern of human inse-
curity and doubt reduces us, and we, in turn, disre-
spect other resources and living things around us.
Lacking esteem for our selves, we struggle to sustain
respect for the rest of God's creations."

— *The Inferiority*

While we don't fully understand life in the present, our teachings and actions suggest that we can piece together the future nonetheless. Some people forecast the end of our world or, more specifically, the end of life on earth. In *The Inferiority*, we don't have "doubtology," but we have eschatology— the study of final events.

Why is there such a pre-occupation to predict the future?

Some people may rationalize that "We need to know so we can plan." However, the above question is critically differ-ent from those of the physical, or corporal, world. It's different because I'm referring to a realm outside of the body and flesh, beyond the here and now, called the extra-corporeal. It may be useful to know how much food to prepare for next month, how much medicine to stock for the next season, or how much space we'll need to house a larger family; these are concerns of the corporeal, or of the body.

Let's contrast the extra-corporal significance like this—Does Life merit its own itinerary?

Is Life inherently worth living, supposing there was no ending? Regardless of the end, we must find applications where we can use our faculties and hone them. Conversely, if we don't employ and improve these faculties, our inaction will produce a negative change.

If there is no ending, I insist that we invariably write one ourselves. Without doubt, the only concern is how it will read. A simplified "ending," or itinerary, essentially outlines a person's birth, growth, and death. By forecasting that we need to feed the flesh, we can stockpile food in the physical itinerary. In the extra-corporal itinerary, we may be more sensitive to anguishing human conditions.

Consider the critical distinction between the corporal and extra-corporal question, suppose we cannot foresee the future. We may have reasons not to stockpile food, but there is no acceptable justification for withholding "sensitivity" among humankind.

While predicting the future might be crucial for physical planning, it only serves to show how selfish our personal aspirations are, in the extra-corporeal.

Therefore, the advantage we seek in the extra-corporal future bears no contribution to the progress of humanity. When is God returning? What does the end of the world look like? Do the good, the bad, and the ugly end up in the same place? How does the appeal process work if there is one? These questions have no part in maturing extra-corporal humans.

A Sunday school teacher rejects the idea that people focus on the end and insists, "Very few actually do." I agree that few consciously make a lifetime profession in the study of final events. Nonetheless, recognized formal religions use precisely the end as a promise and basis for membership.

This promise is made during initiation and throughout the association, and varies in form but can be summed up like this: Obey thy God and thou shall receive salvation— in the end; live now with love and kindness, and ye be granted eternal life— in the end; abandon your material obsessions, so you can attain enlightenment— in the end.

Concurrently, religions warn that sinners, violators, or traitors will be sentenced to hell, torture, or damnation in the end. There is little emphasis on living Life as exemplified by God, so fellow humankind can benefit from the glory of the Almighty. Without the promise of an individual end, the offer doesn't sound quite like a bargain.

We must believe that God expects the return of *Their* children together in humanity— not just opportunists for personal salvation.

For discussion's sake, suppose people can indeed envision or define the future. We inevitably find civilizations with higher degrees of intricacies, more hi-tech marvels, and perhaps more human-removed societies. What capabilities do we have now to analyze, modify, or solidify our current human condition, much less to take advantage of the knowledge of the future?

Let's suppose humans found the code to unlock the gate of heaven.

At about the same time, NATO and its allies have been bombing Yugoslavia for months. India has been conducting air raids against Pakistan, and Iraq's been shooting at United Nation's peace-keeping planes. Additionally, China is likely to possess United States' advance nuclear technology.

If wars don't hit home for some people, how about a different kind of threat— such as genetic cloning? Newspapers reported that corn, which was engineered to produce its own pesticides, is also killing other things such as butterflies. There was also the cloned sheep, Dolly, who aged twice as fast as other sheep, and died prematurely.

We must concede that before long, we might not need to decipher the privileged information, or "the code to unlock the gate of heaven."

The privileged information is probably inscribed in some advanced telepathic format. We simply haven't attained "telepathic" proficiency.

Even though we have the information of the future, what are we prepared to do?

If the future is simpler than our current conditions, we would definitely be able to arm ourselves with the privilege information, you may be thinking. For example, if future medicine is actually less complex, we could administer it today, right?

We can do little in a retrogressive theory, ironically. First, if we continue our course; well, we surely were anyway. If we force-change anything, we will not make it to the enviable future we supposedly predict. If we stop our progress now, there's no way we will get to the point of simplification.

Consequently, if the future is more advanced, we are ill equipped to benefit from its information. If the future is more simplified, we'll be overqualified, maybe— but cannot capitalize on the information either.

I realize there's a stigma on people who live for the day, from hand to mouth, and see only the end of their nose. However strong that stigma is, moving on to the next day, when today is only a blur, is negligent.

Why is there such an occupation about seeing the future? Perhaps what people really want to see is the terminal event, not tomorrow, and not for the responsible planning they may claim.

Do you suppose how we live in Life depends on this knowledge, or lack thereof?

Depending on the ending we may never love, be kind, or lend a hand. I don't believe most of us operate that way. If there were no ending whatsoever, would we completely abolish our value system or enhance it?

Would people stop or wage more wars?

Regardless of other reasons for looking ahead, many of us feel like the world is coming to an end. The new millennium certainly introduces many conclusions about the termination of life, and there are also analysts who suggest that the world will end some years or centuries later. While it is apparent that we will not get an agreement on a specific date, we get a grave sense that the event is very real.

With respect to Life, why do we have such a preoccupation with death and the end?

Maybe many of us are anxious to harmlessly conclude a difficult trial, for Life has been no more than misery, misfortune, and inopportunity. We all probably can feel ill-equipped and untrained, underpowered and apprehensive, uninformed and imperceptive in our lives— in spite of our external appearance.

Some people may want the whistle blown so that they needn't throw in the towel. Although the net result of a disqualifying event and quitting is the same, no one wants to be on record as a quitter. Maybe one too many harsh words was said to a brother, and we don't have to apologize if not given the chance. Some people might have waged war today, and would rather not go through with the threat tomorrow, if tomorrow doesn't come. Someone might have taken the last seat on the train last night, and would rather not see the old lady come Monday?

We are not that lucky.

Not in the year 2000, not 2010, not 2020… Would it shock you if the end of any world will not near for thousands of years more? The calendar could be completely different by then.

We will find that Life does not lap around one clock. Instead, it's an interactive cooperation of multitudes of continuums or dimensions as alluded to in *The Flat Mind*. Consider this: The earth's axis is a line about which human world turns, but our habitual time might not be the axis on which the totality of Life runs.

Instead of predicting and preparing for the end, let us think about restarting the botched New Year's resolution. Maybe the resolution was to finish that technical training or college, to help a poor neighbor, or to get back into physical shape. While taking an eraser to the whiteboard of life can be convenient, we better visit our brother now and retract the threat of force we boasted earlier. Find that train, where you took the last seat, and turn it into a giving exercise.

To appreciate why we look to the end, understand that when people suffer an extended drought, they can only believe that it will rain. The longer into the drought, the stronger the belief, and the more heavily the rain must fall.

It's like the riddle, "How far can you walk into the woods?" Halfway— the other half of the way, you're technically walking out of the woods. Much human strength can be mustered from this riddle, as we garner more optimism for every moment we suffer, that "We'll be out of the woods soon." Alas, this may continue until we perish in resignation.

The certainty of relief, or the end of the world, is not predictable, even though we may study it and yearn for it.

It is clearly written in the scriptures of Judaism, Christianity, and other religions that we would not know when the end comes. This makes mortal sense for if we knew the time, there would be a massive pursuit to superficially "clean house" just before the event. The effect would not be deserving of the end we may anticipate.

This stipulation further dictates that although we cannot predict when the end comes, we know precisely when it does not.

Additionally, people should collectively make the difficult commitment to be coherent when it comes to the use of the Torah, Bible, or any other religious text as propaganda. There is no credibility whatsoever when one source is used as support for two contradicting claims.

For example, the Bible is used to assert that the end of the world will be a complete surprise. People then comb meticulously for evidence between the same covers, to show when it ends.

Aside from "the end," the same texts have been used to pitch differing conclusions about the beginning as well. These examples can be numerous, including a jealous and angry God versus an all-loving God.

We should all be able to decipher this message— live well; God will join us when we have matured. Until then, humankind must realize that we have been using the end, be it afterlife or heaven or hell— to justify the means, or lifestyle. To realize how we use "the end" is to separate once again the corporal and the extra-corporal itineraries.

Paying bills could be an "end" for which we work long hours to provide the "means." Like before, this is a corporal end and differs critically from afterlife, or an extra-corporal end. Paying bills is definitive, but we are inadequate to define "afterlife," or the extra-corporal end. As long as the end is unclear, the means remains vague, and we'll continue to live tentatively at best.

While the end is beyond definition, as afterlife is— the means, or "lifestyle," remains non-committal.

We must rise above laboratory animals whose behaviors strictly follow "the end justifies the means." For these animals, the ends are psychologically conditioned and are clear. Press the pedal three times, and a reward is dispensed; jump through the hoops, and there is a biscuit. You see, these ends are corporal, and these animals are incapable of anything more. Whether animals are capable of anything more may be debatable. The point is there should be no doubt that humans are capable of more than "psychologically conditioned" behaviors.

The Christian Bible states that when God returns to terminate life on earth, *They* better find us doing the work we were commissioned to do.[1] No one can tell you the particulars of your job, but one thing is certain in the message— you're not to be occupied with any investigation into the end of the world.

> *If you want to know your past,*
> *look into your present condition;*
> *if you want to know your future,*
> *look into your present action.*
> — Padmasambha

---

[1] Mathew 24, *King James Bible.*

The Heaven

THE HEAVEN

"While taking an eraser to the whiteboard of life can be convenient, we better visit our brother now and retract the threat of force we boasted earlier. Find that train, where you took the last seat, and turn it into a giving exercise."

— *The Prophets*

Like the origin, heaven can be different places to different people, and even different things at different times. We have debated about heaven throughout the history of humanity, as if it is the main reason for Life.

Congregations from every corner of the world work diligently a lifetime to go to heaven. Scholars, disciples, and bystanders alike, all seem to have taken on a personal interest to define the concept and clarify the picture, as if to somehow help each other find the way.

Thousands of years later, atheists, Buddhists, Christians, Hindus, Jews, Muslims and more, turn heaven into a mysterious endgame. Not only is heaven merely a point of attainment now, we have also reduced the mission of religions. As if without knowing, we belittle the individuals around us— and the One who dwells within.

Our fixation on heaven necessitates yet a new governor of life, where personal prerogatives are veiled from scrutiny, as long as they can be justified with a religious overtone.

The new rule of law seems to allow that as long as my supporting evidence is more dramatic than yours, I can kill you in war, deprive you of opportunities, or unleash my anger in the absence of kindness. For example, if the international allies can assemble a more impressive justification than a sovereign nation, then bombing may commence. That's exactly what NATO and its allies did March 25, 1999, and sustained the bombardment until Yugoslavia turned into ruins.

Yugoslavia was not targeted in the name of heaven, but the situation shows vividly how even killing can be justified in pursuit of an endgame.

"Who or what religion teaches this?" a reader protested. Again, this book is not about any one religion in particular. I am not going to discuss any particular dogmatic curriculum here. Have you not heard that most wars were fought in the name of the Prince of Peace? Do you not know of one religious faith, which condemns another as hell bound?

Perhaps heaven is the final place, or a graveyard of sorts where the dead eventually live on. Others do not focus very much on heaven, but rather on the avoidance of hell. For these people, heaven is a luxury they need not afford, as they accept that avoiding hell is definitely more critical. Within these two groups, the one seems more selfish and the other more humble, but both are self-serving. The former would step on a fellow human to reach heaven— the latter would do the same to hedge hell.

The sad irony of the human portrait lies in the fact that neither the suitors of heaven nor evaders of hell know the object of their envy or fear. As a result, they both scurry haphazardly only to remain within the four sides enclosing the dark canvas. Do you tailor your life for one end or the other? Do your thoughts, actions, and inspirations revolve around reaching heaven or avoiding hell?

Imagine the extent of human travel if it were in the right direction. Can you envision where humankind could be today, after people spent all their resources and wasted all that time?

For many people, anything but earth is heaven, never mind its size or distance. I like to think that heaven must be multitudes grander than earth, but I do understand how, for some people, it does not have to be.

Let's suppose there is a heaven for every faith. Although our expectations of heaven might be markedly different, they all share a commonality. That is, heaven is a better place, dimension, or time compared to the worldly earth we now inhabit.

My wife describes heaven as an altered reality where our post-physical life, its pains, and rewards are realized by our preferences. She believes that if working on computers is my passion, then my heavenly reality would be a life surrounded by computers.

My contemplative father has trouble completing his picture of heaven, but believes it's a place where all standards are raised. Our willpower will be immeasurable, our intellectual capability immense, with a paralleled and inescapable responsibility. It's as if someone moved the first-down marker by 50 yards, or cranked up the heat in the kitchen by 100 degrees.

I don't particularly see a need for detailing what heaven is, for I truly do not have a clue. As emphasized in *The Prophets*, Life must deserve its own itinerary. For example, heaven might end up being a small dimension near Eden's compost pile. It suffices, in this case, to say that I wouldn't like it, and wouldn't enjoy my eternity next to the heap. Should I now turn kindness into self-serving greed, basic fairness into cruel advantage, or prevailing righteousness into wicked pursuit of an endgame?

Do we know how humanity will arrive at heaven, or do we simply know about our personal arrivals there?

While we cannot determine heaven for sure until we get there, we should be very certain of what we expect from its new inhabitants.

Then there are people who insist that there is no such thing as heaven. I will show later that perhaps the prescribed ideas of heaven thus far have not found an accord with yours. Maybe everyone describes heaven as a physical place or an approachable time— and for you, heaven is a state of the soul where the mind can't quite comprehend. In disagreeing with others' idea of heaven, I insist that you must have found your own. It's from this idea, or stance, that you hold your opposition to others' notions of heaven.

You might not even realize that you have a stance. You're simply repelled from those who carry on with presumptions. By persistently refusing to partake in their claims, you have necessarily constructed an idea to overcome their improbable notion, and a defense to your alternate possibility. At least you still uphold, in reverence, the One who lives within. You represent certain energy, and your conclusion of a heaven is likely not the void you might suggest.

I can see how you do not want to be like others, but do not let them decide that you should end in emptiness. Deny what others claim or push onto you, and deny their reasoning, purpose, or endgame. Don't take your dismissal overboard lest you should deny yourselves the multitudes of magnificent possibilities. You are entitled. You are endowed. You are empowered.

No God will override your option to reject heaven, or to stay behind— for your decision is final.

I want to impress upon you another thought. While our body can be severed and can bleed, we are more than the flesh from which our weaknesses come. I insist that our body, or physical nature, is but one characteristic of our entire being. We must be emotional, spiritual, mental, and psychological, as we are physical. Perhaps we also are many more "dimensional-selves" than we know.

The physical "self" is not the entire you, any more than the spiritual or the emotional self. When a limb is severed, it ceases to exist in the physical world. When people die, we can no longer visit them or embrace them as before. In the absence of the limb, the body lives on. In the absence of the flesh, we too will live on.

Your life will not conclude with the same dark emptiness as can be found at the end of a theatrical masterpiece. You will not be able to indulge yourself at the end of your journey with the luxury of the nothingness for which you wait all of your life.

French philosopher Jean Paul Sartre may argue that nothingness really is "the end." Without getting into Sartre's existentialism and atheistic doctrines, we must look to "consistency" as the one basic test that theories must pass to remain viable. At a fundamental level, existentialism conceives that individual physical existence takes precedence over abstract, conceptual essence.

Moreover, it states that humans are totally free and responsible for their acts. A brief examination shows that existentialist principles fail our consistency test. While physical existence can be very tangible, there is nothing concrete about "responsibility." Additionally, choice is emphasized as a founding existentialist principle, in many literary works. Whether choice is defined loosely or otherwise— it, too, is very abstract.

When a tree dies, the energy that once sustained it continues to sustain life, albeit other life. When a glass of wine is empty, the pleasure of the vintage continues beyond the aftertaste. At a rudimentary level, do organ donors die in "emptiness" when their liver or heart sustains someone else?

What if I am wrong, and there is no heaven?

You assess the consequence!

What if you are wrong, and there is heaven?

If you don't believe in heaven, the penalty for your disbelief is another life void of complete fulfillment, as you carry it out once again as a spectator in [your] heaven. The only thing people can do when presented with such an awesome and foreign reality, someday, is to continue in disbelief.

Understanding the penalty, believing and preparing for heaven seem like the only *responsible* alternative.

Whether we choose to arrive better prepared than the last time— we will carry on.

It is good to have an end to journey toward;
but it is the journey that matters, in the end.
— Ursula K. Le Guin

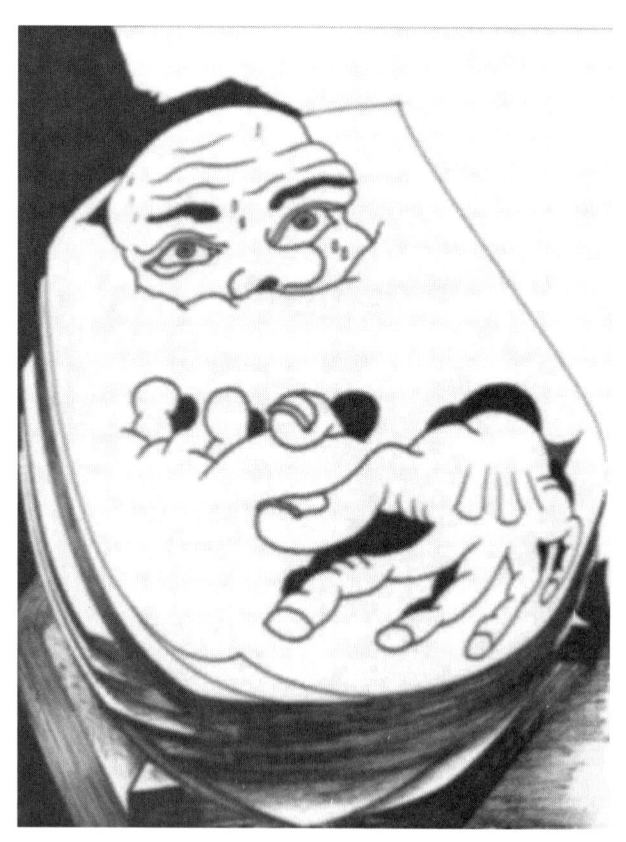

The Dogma

THE DOGMA

"No one has ever challenged us as to who our parents are, even though some people may have unique family circumstances. We only need to introduce and claim our parents once, be they adoptive or biological.

Consequently, who is disputing about the Parents *in your life?"*

— *The Monkey*

Whether atheists, Buddhists, Christians, Hindus, Jews, Muslims, or others, we were born into this world with no choice of our own. I don't recall agreeing to come into this world as a helpless baby, a trying teenager, or a fail prone adult. No one asked me if I wanted to be a boy or a girl. I wasn't given the chance to be a bird of prey like an eagle, or a king of beasts like a lion.

You were not consulted about the life you undertake, or the challenges you face. We can't negotiate our strengths, weaknesses, assignment, or timing on earth. While many of us are in one way or another luckier than the rest, it's no consolation if we're better off in areas that, to us, don't matter. I am gifted at this but, frankly, I would rather be good at what you do. Maybe you have too much of one thing, but lack something else.

We don't want everything. What we do want is what fits our life and challenges.

Would we be ungrateful?

Ungratefulness is merely a symptom of equity gone wrong. Conversely, gratefulness is a rationale we resort to when faced with a no-alternative situation. It's not too surprising that we need to rehearse for so long before acquiring the awkward "ability." Gratefulness just isn't natural.

Giving me things that don't work or that I cannot get to work is inequitable and ineffective, to say the least. It's not an issue of social etiquette or spiritual mannerism, but of functional suitability. If we are judged on our patriotism then provide us the combative means. If we are scored on our ability to thwart evil, then allow us to train for such a challenge. If we are measured as to how much fear we can disguise, then all we need is practice.

Are you perfectly endowed? If not, have you been entirely honest?

Please don't make me inadequate for my assignment on earth, then challenge me to be mature, thankful, and sincere at the same time.

If God gave me a short leg, I'm not going to like it. I have an obligation to communicate it plainly. If I were created specifically to patrol mountainsides where a shorter leg helps me walk better along the upper side of an incline, I can appreciate that. Otherwise, all I'm doing is filtering my inherent dismay through a dogmatic converter to ultimately produce insincere thanks and praises.

"You're not being fair to God," some people might point out, "We just don't understand God's plans." Even if this is the case, God remains the all-knowing God. The majority of people don't get the message, or comprehend much of it. Not only must we define our own tools before we can begin God's work, must we decode the mission from God-speak?

Oh? Perhaps our job is a surprise, and the tools come from within us. After all, most people like surprises, and it's convenient if the tools are only an arm's length inside. Is the tool called faith by chance? I hope this doesn't take away your fire, but humankind has been forging this faith, or tool, for a few thousands years now. It's disappointing that all we have accomplished thus far is an intelligent race that survives on for-geries, if you will.

We are children of a deliberate God and our assignment is by a lottery system or, as many people call it, by surprise. If we are expected to come up with the tool required, in addition to finishing the job, it must have been apparent to God from the onset that we might not get the job done.

Either we have a messed up God, or humans have con-strued Life terribly wrong for thousands of years.

Certainly many people have quite a wonderful life, as some people appear to have everything. We consider ourselves blessed, with some job security and a nice home. For nearly all of us, regardless of how many material possessions we have, somewhere in our lives a painful void exists. So big and bitter is this cavity that some of us can't even visit it for fear the tight rope we walk will snap, consuming us and all we've managed to balance so tenderly.

We have mitigated our perceived inequities with self-consolations like "You can't have everything," and "You win some, you lose some." The fact is, consoling ourselves is all we can do realistically, is it not? We have no choice about how the hand of Life is dealt.

It seems we are inevitably staged for failure, however diligently we might rehearse. We were born without options, given an inconspicuous job by lottery, furnished no tools, and told to come up with them ourselves— otherwise just wing it.

How can Life ever be fair if this is how it starts? Have we construed everything wrong, or is God playing with us?

The Human Struggle will illuminate some answers. One thing to keep in mind is that the fundamental premises, around which our lives revolve, determine how we perceive Life. Understood or not, it's difficult to tell after several thousand years if people have misconstrued Life from the beginning. Nevertheless, we have one reliable system— the consistency test. Can a premise, claim, or law in question be consistent across applications?

Let me illustrate one such premise. While we may complain that our birth was without choice, our parents would have argued that some decision or choice was indeed made. "We decided to have a baby," they insist. We casually accepted this notion as far back as it began, at universal, societal, and personal levels, yet we haven't really reflected upon it.

What do people mean when they say, "We decided"? When two people make love, the generally expected result is a pregnancy or a baby on the way. Humans can disrupt the established reproductive laws and destroy the forthcoming life, but we cannot willfully decide for or against it.

Life is not our decision— unless we are confusing the issues.

We do not control natural conception. There is no choice, no arbitration. People of all ages know, at least privately, how little we control when it pertains to Life. For thousands of years, cultures have acknowledged this, as evident by enlisting gods and spirits. People have long needed superhuman help to intervene in the deliberation of Life.

Consequently, claiming: "We decided to have children," or "We're going to hold off" is one premise that people have misconstrued for a long time. I understand what this customarily means, but it's still not excusable that many of us become accustomed to human notions, without thoughtfulness to God.

When we lay down to sleep at night, we must know that children do not come to us merely by our power of lust and desire, but rather by God's design. We may decide to mate— but Life is signed off only by God.

After birth, we must wait for physical growth, and to eventually become consciously cognizant. Then most of us are taught, in various ways, that the life we live is temporary; our bodies aren't really ours, and that we shouldn't get too intimate or reliant on them. Supposedly, our lives are merely those of pre-butterfly caterpillars, destined for the real thing some day, somewhere, but not yet, not here.

Consequently, our preoccupation with the life "after" begins.

As I discussed in *The Heaven*, we all have ideas about the real life, or the life after. We believe we'll live the "life after" in a more or less perfect place. We haven't thought about a more developed human race though. Historically, it's been easier expecting a perfect place than working for a more perfect self.

The more we see how temporary this world is, the more we realize we cannot miss the eternal one.

It seems that we no longer need to be clouded by the inequity of our birth, as it fades from our forethoughts. We needn't be confused about what God wants us to do, because we now have a self-prescribed mission. Unlike the one God may have assigned from the lottery, the new mission before us is clear. This one is not fueled by novelty, popularity, nor charity, but by a personal fire to attain that one life— which the one we're living should have been.

People have continued this mission for thousands of years oblivious to the irony. Although we began without a choice to life, then were placed only in a temporary one, most of us now believe an afterlife is possible just on the other side of death. With a purpose, believers are willing to pay with their lives and posterity. At least, part time.

We all have "full-time" jobs doing something else. After all, people spend more time on youth soccer, football, cellular phones, magazines, and just about any other interests, than working at this afterlife campaign.

Deep down inside, we want to put in just enough effort so that we can collect the prize, regardless of the level of importance we assign to afterlife. If we are sold on eternal life as a rising "stock," why the broad portfolio? While diversifying financial investment is strategic, with God, aren't we saying *They* are overrated? What percentage of our resources is allocated to this vested interest of afterlife?

Why diversify— why dance the spiritual line? Why dance the lines of good and bad, real giving and charity, truths and lies?

How many beggars can I shake off before I lose my take? How many confessions do I skip before I turn into the sin? When do disguises of duty exempt me from having compassion? At what point does God take notice? While our questions go unanswered, we look to mishaps, or bad luck, big and small throughout our lives and interpret them as God's signs.

To perpetuate the afterlife notion, moreover, and to regulate spiritual conducts, humans did something shocking. Our forefathers institutionalized our relationship with God and called it religion.

God became an ordained concept, a social order, another classification in human lives.

Shortly thereafter came books and songs, rules and regulations, office hours and times of worship. Teaching was introduced across the landscape, and people were taught systematically how to have a relationship with God— now called "religion." When to pray and what to say, as well as to whom one must pray, have become integral parts of this education. We are also taught what to believe and, equally important, how to give thanks or, at least, to do it often. What and how we sing were also formalized. The regime soon became hierarchical, and ensuing complications have not relented.

Formalized "religion" permeates every aspect of our lives, big and small, public and private. To whom should we give and, of course, how much or when. What are we to sacrifice, in which manner, and for how long. For example, many religions use fasting as a sacrificial token. As it was before "religion" began, many people straddle spiritual lines.

Some people are not supposed to eat pork during fasting. Veterans might say, don't worry. There are ways to fry up some mouth-watering string beans. There are ways to really dress up fish. Who says anyone should give up flavor, right? What happens if we don't eat pork in the first place? Well, we've banked so many days of devotion with God that we'll never need to fast again, although we might fast partially to support family or friends.

While we're at it, why not add a special request or two. It's like going to the tailor, since we are doing errands anyhow. Some of us openly bargain with God for our sacrifice. I will deprive myself a little more than everyone else, and please get me that new raise. I'll even suffer a bit more than religion calls for, if you can just make sure my mother goes to heaven.

An irreversible process to mechanize a divine relationship has mistakenly begun.

Maybe we never really had a relationship with God before. Now, though, we are sure we have religion. This institution operates, as many institutions do, habitually, and involuntary like a reflex.

We don't treat our parents as an establishment. We do not regimen our love with them and rationalize it to our friends and ourselves. We do not ask for things using parrot-talk or reciting give-me books. We don't make our thanks genuine by using sanctified plagiarism. I trust you share the comfort we embrace in our relationship with our families, next of kin, and friends. Our families are integral parts of our lives, and we are integral parts of theirs.

I suspect that in the beginning no one could have contemplated the ramifications of formalizing the human-God relationship. Nonetheless, everyone participated, not just spiritual leaders, thinkers, and lawmakers. Because one institution can't work for all people, we find ourselves with many denominations, religions, and gods. Now, it seems the only truth is that we have a quick readiness to disagree. Worse yet, "we agree to disagree."

It's like secularism at the highest severity. Instead of going from "church" to world, or heavenly to worldly, or holy to profane, people institutionalize the profound communion—and bring about religion.

Our relationship with God weighs in less than a family tradition now; granted, different geographical areas and religious faiths don't all scale the same. Traditions such as hunting and fishing, physical and mental sports, or something subtler like cooking and wine-making, all draw us closer to their essences. It's if our lives consist of these age-old traditions and a great many more, while religion is just an insurance policy.

Do we jump out of bed in the morning because we're going to visit with God today, or because it's harvest time in the vineyard? We're careful to formally thank God when we celebrate with a toast, but can we feel God's delight when we have pleasure? Do we have the courage to ingest a delectable glass of the best for God, or do we assume *They* drink from the shrine we constructed aside from the orchestra of life?

Institutionalizing our relationship with God was a mistake, indicative of an incomplete deliberation by the human thinking machine in haste. Nobly, we are to renounce material possessions and pick up the ways of a holy life. However, we end up renouncing one another in pursuit of personal salvation.

Besides "mechanizing a divine relationship," the march to be holier-than-thou begins under the veil of religious duty. History shows that people readily subjugate others for personal righteousness. You don't think we're that lame, or you can't believe that I'm suggesting it? Consider this damning assertion— "Only followers of our faith are going to heaven." If you don't start worshiping our god, you'll burn in hell.

"No one is like that anymore." Some people may feel that people accept everyone now. Moderation is good, but how do we realistically get to one end— heaven or afterlife— by standing around in the middle?

If you don't see the spiritual dance coming, perhaps you're too accustomed to it.

For such a long time, we have refused to say there's a right and a wrong answer, after failed centuries of hard-line intolerance. We realize how a hard line cannot achieve the greater reception and broader membership. Tolerance means patience, constructive pro-action, and judgmental restraint. Instead of taking a right or wrong stance, with "judgmental restraint," we have been hugging the gray areas in the middle to be sympathetic and accommodating.

There is a way to have a relationship with God, and it's not by observing or practicing religion. There is a way to afterlife, and there is a way to eternal death. Each person might be entitled to his or her opinion, but a relationship with God is not a gray line.

We have many gray lines now certifying the conviction of people who are serious moderates. We add increasingly more gray lines every time we confuse flexibility, which bends both ways, with tolerance. The drive for tolerance requires earnest work, in contrast to the flexibility pretense, where "That's your opinion, I have mine."

As a virtue in countless aspects of life, flexibility does no more than perpetuate the human spiritual dance. Suppose an individual does not recognize God as our supreme *Parents*, we might hear a rationalization like, "Times are different now, we can't discriminate." Entitlement becomes more important than truth.

Look, friends. While human-made extremes can be moderated to include *everyone*, we cannot use pseudo-truths to attain eternal life.

There can be much tolerance in the way we communicate the Truth, and in our treatment of one another. Our delivery of the message and our patience for a candid response are some areas we must modify— not the message or the Truth. We must take time to communicate and understand each other. For instance, until I understand you, I must submit that I don't yet understand, and work toward understanding, but not pass you off by saying, "It's your opinion."

It's not our decision that a stamp of entitlement [to an opinion] should suffice for the Truth, merely because we're eager to move on. "We need to be flexible," should mean you and I— not righteousness— must be flexible.

Consequences of the misappointed flexibility virtue are plainly apparent now. We can no longer discern one gray line from another, be it political, social, ethical, economical, psychological, physical, mental, or technological. Perhaps we could combine these gray lines into a large gray matter and call it the big brain.

In varying severity, we've been living in a new era of permissive correctness, in the name of tolerance religiously, socially, politically, and otherwise. To be clear, this is flexibility confused and disguised as tolerance. We grow flexible to passively weather life's defiant contests, like laden wheat wavering wearily in the storm.

It takes courage and maturity to distinguish human adaptation— and the Truth.

Notwithstanding its pretenses, harping on the flexibility notion might not be fair, because many cultures don't even as much as pretend to be flexible. They simply do not care to excuse their ungodly intolerance. Not being able to find resolutions among people, it is unfortunate that humans should persecute because of our differences. We must celebrate the fact that being different is inherent to our divine design.

How do we maintain that there is one God and, at the same time, genuinely accept everyone?

We must set our priorities straight. Foremost, we need to re-examine our conviction for eternal life. Next, we must determine the one single requirement to meet for "eternal life" to be a mere possibility. Realize that if we ineptly close the door on the opportunity, we forfeit any subsequent chance to achieve our priorities.

That single requirement is communion, or an intimate relationship with deep understanding, with God.

It's not very complicated, as it mustn't be, but only pure devotion to the cause can sustain the challenge. It's not only communion with God, but also with each other. Make communion the governor of our activities, hobbies, and entire life.

Make communion our new priority, and leave that human-made contraption called dogma in schools.

Listen to others. If no one is talking, we can ask questions— then listen. Ask a Buddhist, how does a person *awaken* oneself? Ask a Muslim, how does a person *surrender* to God? Ask a Hindu, how does yoga *unite* people with the Almighty? Ask a Christian, was sin the only price that Jesus paid? When you cannot relate, ask others to explain and demonstrate. When given the chance, speak plainly. Have others echo your voice where you are not understood. Maybe what we say is not comprehendible. Maybe what we articulate never leaves the confines of our minds.

We cannot have true communion with God, if we cannot understand each other.

How else can we afford the consistency or coherence required to take a definitive position— heaven or hell, right or wrong, or we versus they— realizing we cannot attain eternal life by straddling two realms?

People figured out a way to take a definitive position a long time ago. Entirely reject one of the two realms. Rejecting evil, and specifically its ruler, has become humankind's oldest occupation.

Dogma instated a vigorous campaign to reject Satan, or the devil, as a part of human religion. Not only do people have a misconstrued tolerance notion, we now face an irreversible, self-imposed task of deciding good and evil. We haven't learned what, who, or how to tolerate, and now— to reject.

Religions, their books, and teachers require us to renounce the devil and his evil work. Unfortunately, not religions, books, nor teachers have trained us to identify the devil, who we vow to renounce. Yet, we have grown by our own presumptuous power to incriminate with certainty. We might have suspicions about the identity of God, but most people would claim to know evil when they see it. We may question God's authorship, yet we recognize the workmanship of the devil at a glance.

Nations, cultures, and regimes can reject their fellow members swiftly. People can convict each other with harsh judgments, because the suspects might resemble the work of hired hands. In fact, our brothers and sisters in humanity are the only ones we reject. Sometimes people insist that they can even identify individuals belonging to us but employed by Satan.

At least the familiar images make up the devil we need to expose, because we are unable to really catch Satan himself. It's clear from history that the need to reject Satan triumphs over the recognition of kindred members of the same human race.

Not only does dogma teach us to win, it expects us to win, hence the creation of war and defeat.

Satan is not impressed with our fight. We might not know how many evil soldiers Satan has, but we should have an idea of how many human comrades we have felled over time, across borders, and within homes. How many more friendly casualties will there be before we figure out that Satan is not the one we have been eliminating? After thousands of years, he remains.

Let's take notice that we have been felling our own.

To realize this is to understand that the miseries the world suffers are humanly attributable. I suspect that might sound cliché to many people, but do humans really have a mechanism to isolate the devil's work— as opposed to the work of an ailing brother or sister? We are pompous fools if we think that we have been thwarting the forces of Satan.

"Do you think Hitler was evil, or a fine brother?" a faithful Christian protests. Please stick with the issue. I am not suggesting that some people can't be despicable, or evil. If I pulled the trigger and killed someone, that is my ugliness. Whether I acted alone or with Satan, humankind is not advanced enough to discern. Until people can really distinguish the work of the devil, we must not play judge and jury.

Joan of Arc was no Hitler. Nonetheless, her countrymen, fueled by their religious beliefs, burned her at the stake as a heretic, for they only knew how to reject. Years later, they assumed their own authority and made Joan of Arc a saint.

This book is not about Hitler or Joan of Arc, but it is precisely about our pledge to renounce, and our inability to tell the difference.

Do we seriously understand Satan or his powers, from any faith? Do you, your religion, and its teachers soberly believe you can withstand a physical, much less spiritual, blow from Satan?

Some people may contend that Satan, the ruler of the underworld, is the one who causes us to confuse and stray. Be realistic. We first must reach his spiritual elevation, before we can attract him. As long as we're spiritually disorientated, we haven't as much as entertained him. It's like the entire human race walking around in bee protective suits for thousands of years, and have yet to scale the heights to the hives.

"Reject the devil. Renounce Satan!" The human religions decry. This renunciation includes the chance, however prudent, that Satan is not even involved. Without a definite spiritual alignment, who and how many we displace or reject becomes the signature of membership for many people.

Have you thought about what institution could answer so directly and so effectively to the selfish chambers of the human heart? What institution can be so big and loud and forceful, yet so subtle, communicable, and single-handedly successful?

Notwithstanding, how do we deny darkness and uphold the light? We get serious!

Do humans have the conviction to renounce the devil? Do we have the physical, mental, and spiritual equipment to do the job, realistically? Perhaps what people have really meant for the last millennia is, instead of developing and becoming capable victors, we simply want to be instruments of God. Many people believe that who they become and what they do are God's direct will. In *The Human Struggle*, we will look at dogma's instrumentation notion, and how it permeates in our lives.

Recognize the constructions of dogma— schools, communities, even families. This recognition is vital because, "I was taught wrong" will not be an acceptable excuse before God. Following doctrines irresponsibly will not be a good alibi for our absent *flat mind*.

To eliminate Satan is also to control the temptation to classify God and the devil as good and evil, or light and darkness. Otherwise, we trivialize our Almighty God. This is minimizing because the devil and his evil are in themselves simple and singular, while God on the other hand is everything comprehensively that has and has not been.

These are not two equal-but-opposite forces, but necessarily a prevalent Force versus a petty corruptive one.

We must understand that God does not share the other side of the coin with the devil, as our casual language and religious cultures suggest. This is not a 50-50 toss— but an eventual and certain eclipse by God and *Their* creations.

If we live with the understanding and certainty that God's creations will eclipse Satan, the devil or demons, dogma could no longer strike fear or acquire compliance. If we do not juggle tolerance and rejection, we would not straddle the realms of heaven and hell, good and bad, and we versus they. True communion is then possible.

Once we have learned to commune, our relationship with God does not have to be elaborate, mechanical, or superfluous. We will understand why Life is not something humankind can author, and why the circumstances of our births are not explainable with suppositions constructed by dogma. Religious rationales will cease to perplex us, for our communion precipitates a higher understanding.

Let us now tend to the sensitive task of understanding and defending the concept of life and death, which according to instituted religions and their dogmas— is temporary.

> *The only thing that interferes with my learning is*
> *my education.*
> — Albert Einstein

The Paper Plate

THE PAPER PLATE

Recognize the constructions of dogma— schools, communities, even families. This recognition is vital because, "I was taught wrong" will not be an acceptable excuse before God. Following doctrines irresponsibly will not be a good alibi for our absent flat mind.

— The Dogma

Whether people believe Life is deliberate or anything less, its permanency is a point around which human actions revolve. While scholars may argue that permanence depends on how "Life" is defined, I leave it to you to define Life personally. However arrived, your and my definitions of Life have little to do with what it ultimately is.

Life defines itself.

We may say that people discover and present descriptions of Life. That is, we must understand that descriptions can describe, but definitions cannot define what we didn't "engineer." Let's say we describe Life, but let's not think we define Life— for we do not.

We can only perceive Life, cooperate with it, and react to it. Appreciating this premise is critical to forming our thoughts, which then shape our entire being. It's critical because our thoughts govern not only our lives, but also those of generations who inherit our cultures. In turn, our resulting mindset dictates how we perceive Life. Without due care, the circle of perception-mindset-perception can make us unfit to comprehend Life and its conditions.

One condition is that people can die from illnesses, accidents or, old age. Since the beginning of human history, people have inferred that life's temporary because we all die, as evident in the social and religious cultures today. Religious dogma also made a persistent case that this life is temporary. Because this is one of the founding premises of human life, we must understand its profound impact on humanity.

What does "temporary" mean?

It is a measure of being or existence relative to time. Traditionally, as long as we can measure something, people call it finite or temporary.

Human time fundamentally depends on the earth orbiting the sun, giving us night and day, or a 24-hour cycle. What would happen if the sun shone everywhere, such that we never have dusk, darkness, or dawn? Time would not be a valid measure from the beginning.

Obviously, the sun is not everywhere— but God is!

While our physical, or corporal, orbit circles the sun, where should our extra-corporal orbit revolve?

Imagine that we each have our own timeline. After all, our lives do have different commencements and graduate independently in time. To function together, we have agreed to work off the same clock hanging on the wall. While we must cooperate with this common timeline, it is not a unified one. Our individual lives, above the societal level, continue on our personal time gradients. This simply means that we each have our own temporal rhythm, metabolic rate, or biological clock.

We expect that each individual is different physically, mentally, psychologically, physiologically, and spiritually. Yet, we willingly believe one clock can tick for all of us. More alarmingly, we believe that the human clock can tell time for all creation. Some time ago, we had an earth-centered universe, and now— human-centered time.

Let's look at time from a different perspective. Suppose life cycles around a *discordometer* where, as long as I am happy, the numbers do not increment as in a car's odometer at rest. Every time I feel a discord or a disagreement, the meter reading accelerates. What we would have is a new measuring tool, the *discordometer*, as well as a variable with some significance to us.

With the *discordometer*, is life temporary?

Suppose for the new millennium, the church engineers a new meter to clock our conductivity with God like electricity in metals. Consistent with our philosophy, we measure a constructive entity, which is conductivity in this case. Do I live as long as I'm connected, or conducting?

What is the moral of the clock stories?

What is temporary or permanent: discord, disconnection, or the body?

What are we measuring? If in all our vast endowment of ingenuity and intelligence, we can only measure the flesh then, frankly, we are not ready to understand permanence, eternity, or Truth.

The body on this earth might be temporary— Life is not!

Living a physical life with finite limitations is delicately different from incompletely living one. This delicate distinction is the underlying governor for our inherent ability and willingness to adapt to changing needs and circumstances.

This delicate distinction also is the governor for our thinking machine, and seamlessly weaves every pattern of our fabric of life. We guard this fabric with our pride and defend it with our integrity and wit. We embrace what we have become, as well as how we have come to be, at any cost, whether we are conscious of the price. For instance, if prearranged marriage were a "way" we embrace, we would defend it at an expense greater than our children's merriment. Right or wrong, defendable or not, it's as if our traditional statues, or governor, cannot be attacked.

Our pledge to defend this "fabric" goes beyond our children's well-being, and permeates our relationship with God. An example would be how we continually lament death, a *way* that has become a part of us— at the price of completely missing the Life that we cannot afford to miss. That's not to mention the *way* different faiths and denominations condemn one another at the cost of denying God, who lives in all of us.

Our principles and ideologies will be tried, while the governor confuses tradition with truth. Until one unfortunate day when our sacred and unquestioned life in the "holodeck" is severely refuted, we remain faithful only to the governor. Usually, the awakening is a shock devastating to our thinking machine and adaptive animal. The result is a feeble submission of human frailty. It's like a ruptured egg yolk or a shattered mirror that slips out from under our tried and true grip.

Consider the five o'clock news before the fireplace or the dawn-breaking papers behind a steaming cup of coffee. Somewhere, a man unsuspectingly strikes, hunting his children through the woods, murdering his wedded wife, and despicably kills himself.

Some people would argue that such tragedies are a result of genetic disposition and the environment, while others would blame politicians, gun manufacturers, work, and school. We should be concerned about what makes up this person's value system, what conflicts does he have within it, what caused the conflicts, and how many people share similar values and circumstances.

As another incomprehensible refute, a young immigrant mother of six meditatively strangled all life out of her young children, all six of them. The pain will be haunting and excruciating, as her suicide attempt failed, leaving her to bear the consequences alone. Though inclined to empathize with her tribulations as fellow humans, some people subtly wonder if she has been living in the *holodeck* too long. What kind of "little world" did society, culture, and dogma help landscaped in her mind?

Maybe it was that "governor" at work weaving subtle fabric of life. Maybe it was the "critical distinction" between living a life that ends one day, and temporarily living one.

Think about our attitude toward a temporary job. I may have good work ethics, but I'm not going to plan for any permanent goal, or contemplate anything lasting. I know this temporary job will dispose of me eventually and, maybe, without warning or explanation. I do not have an environment in which to build good relationships or a lasting career.

How different is it if I'm a permanent employee— but have a temporary mindset?

To correct our taught temporary tendencies, we need to live with accountability. Life is found on the journey, the permanent journey. "Permanent" is critical because, as long as we're talking about Life, we require an on-going journey. The moment we plan for our own finish— we forfeit Life. Henceforth, we live painstakingly a life long for the end, which is now meaningless.

There are scriptures that state simply that we will not live in our bodies on this earth forever. What they have been advising for thousands of years is there are additions to Life for which we must prepare.

The way we perceive Life helps form our mindset, which in turn governs how we perceive Life. This cycle of perception can elevate us, or confine us along with succeeding generations.

When it comes to educating children, parents tell them that nothing is forever, "Don't dwell in it!" Children sometimes ask, "Why do people build things that break?" as they don't accept that anything could be gone. Something always possesses us at this point to say things like, "Life is temporary."

As with other practices, we institute our tentative fabric of life into family cultures— to remember, to preserve, and to educate. One day when asked, "Why do people die?" we each have our own evasive answer.

Many people might defend that we are protecting our children from seeing, feeling, or fearing death. Our kids should not know that people grow old, may fall ill, and die. Are we trying to preserve an impression that Life is timeless, forever— or permanent, ironically?

Have you ever wondered how children start out with such a permanent belief and expectation of Life?

Somewhere in us, are there feelings at odds with each other? We live Life temporarily or tentatively, but expect our children to carry on in timelessness or permanence?

Whether or not people can handle dying, they need to toughen up or, at least, give the children a valid answer. While old age and sickness often kill us, sometimes we die more violently. Whether we die from illness or recklessness, we must not blame it on God.

If a student drank too much and killed his friends, then we need to face up with the tragedy and tell the truth. "Honey, the Lord called them home," doesn't suffice. Even if God did, there is still a more imminent truth as pertained to our corporal life on earth. It's imminently true that the student drove his friends to their deaths in gross negligence.

That truth is someone's son has killed someone else's children with his learned irresponsibility. Perhaps he has been kept from knowing that people can die, ironically, while his parents raise him up in a temporary world.

The certainty of this "imminent truth" demands precedence over our speculation that, somewhere else, maybe God turned the wheel. This imminent truth is exactly what our children should hear.

Your life, my life, and our children's lives are permanent as long as we live them. Irresponsibility, though, can change all of that. When people get old or ill, and die, that's old age and physical death. It has nothing to do with the permanency of Life.

Although I might not want to deal with a tremendous loss, I cannot cowardly lay it on God to obscure the pain, or allow me the self-deceit. We cannot advance as superior beings by eluding our responsibility when confronted with bitter circumstances. Until we live true lives, our whims will always be overshadowed as cowardly attempts to manipulate responsibilities and cast blames. We deprive ourselves, consequently, of yet another opportunity for superiority.

You see, Life is both deliberate and permanent.

The "critical distinction" between living with limitations and living tentatively governs the fabric of our lives. More specifically, this distinction outfits us with a vital faculty to live not only personally, but also interpersonally.

To discover this vital faculty, let's put the issue of permanency aside for a moment, and suppose you have no choice but to live forever. For symmetry and fairness reasons, the enemies you vow to defeat also never die, and the friends you promised to lend a hand to will wait enduringly. It follows that you now must live with your successes and failures for eternity, as if "accountability" is the only valid meter of achievement.

Some people welcome the extra time, to finish old projects and catch up with old friends, while others fear that their ugly past will catch up with them and consume them. Debts can bankrupt us from inside, whether someone collects or not.

Imagine how all people and cultures would stop and change course.

No matter where people are in life, where they plan to be in their careers, or how they spend free time, it all must change. Additionally, these are peaceful and positive changes, driven from internal energies. There is no mandate, no violation, no citation, and no sin. It's an instinctive desire deriving from the need to experience the "permanent journey." The changes might be external and physical initially, but eventually they become patterns of a different fabric.

This fabric will last longer on the time clock, withstand more discords on the *discordometer*, and represent a more permanent communion with God on the measure of conductivity.

Would you abuse your health if you were to live forever? How about your teeth? Would you still shrug off your mom when she tells you not to chew on ice? The rest of your body, how many fingers are you going to find the next time you check? How much sunburn would you risk? Tobacco, alcohol, and drugs, we are talking about doing some serious time here.

Imagine living in conditions we bring about— forever. How many warnings will you ignore?

Let us not forget about the enemies. How would you go about destroying them? Wait! Like you, they live forever.

Historically speaking, when we take out the sword, a life is cut short. When we pull the trigger, someone hits the ground. Every time we insult a neighbor, a community tie snaps. For whichever reasons we engage in maiming, killing, and disfiguring our kind, the larger picture of humanity is the same irrespective of victory or defeat.

That is, we fell only our own.

While we take comfort that a certain battle, or principle, was won over, the makeup of our conflicts starkly stand. With the corpse of the opposed now fallen, we lose the physical evidence of the growing issues, and presume they have been eliminated. Using guns and bombs, words and insults, we cause injuries to those in whom we affix perceived conflicts.

Let me borrow a scene from the metropolitan police department— the combative shooting gallery, where law enforcement officers measure their skills and progress. This is where officers unleash their fury at mockup villains, while restraining from maiming defenseless civilians. A villain drops dead or flops over every time it's hit, leaving only a cutout silhouette or a small swirl of dust on the way down. From time to time, mock women, children, and innocent bystanders are taken down accidentally in these exercises.

Downed hostile targets are celebrated while collateral casualties are regretted, but business in the police department continues. With one push of a button, hostile and friendly targets all pop back up, ready for the next simulation.

Many people have been taking pride in victories for centuries. With swords and shields, we cut one another down.

With planes and bombs, we defoliate each other's lives and reveal our barbarism. With words and insults, we strip people of human dignity. With our blindness, we think we save ourselves from a monster every time someone drops to the ground.

As with the combat gallery, the silhouettes remain after the slaying, as if they signify the original conflicts. They stand squarely, still, after we fell our brothers and sisters. People have erected many victory flags on mountains and molehills—but human conflicts remain a volcanic threat.

Unlike the shooting gallery, however, we cannot resurrect people who died or were immeasurably harmed. We wonder sometimes if good can ever prevail?

Look at whom we maim.

Notwithstanding the human propensity historically, I believe we can all assemble and agree on a constructive tool. What else would people do but promote each other, if everyone believed that we all live forever— if there's no way to eliminate one another?

No way?

Must "no way" be a handicap, or can it be proactive planning? People have invented, endorsed, and instituted many notions throughout history. Can we draft an agreement, whereby "there's no way to eliminate one another"?

Let's devote several hundred years, or however long it takes, to build a foundation knowing what we know of tried alternatives.

Should it matter whether our enemies live forever, even though it might seem more now like they do?

People plan to get old, weak, and helpless, and figure that extra effort will be wasted when their terminal moment comes to bear. It's like a child at the county fair. She has 50 tokens to spend as she plans on the rides to end at 10 o'clock. She paces herself, probably with a few breaks in between to pad the time, so that she can be entertained as close as possible to the end. One thing she will not do is stop with tokens still in hand. She might even finish all of them a bit early, ensuring that she gets her entertainment value before she must go home.

For another child, the rides never really end. For her, there is no countdown anxiety. She may even go home early after sharing her tokens with someone else. She, too, has fun even though she does not make it to many rides. Little does she know that she does not truly exhaust her tokens. By sharing with others, she reinvests her otherwise finite portion. She has a fulfilling day without calculating her finish and focusing only in making the time.

For this child, the rides go on in her dreams as she sleeps that night, and their memories live in her every time she helps bring a smile to yet someone else. For this child, Life is the journey— the permanent journey.

Do you live your life with tokens? More precisely, do you live a token life?

What possibility would people rule out when they're capable of the concept of a permanent Life?

Think permanent.

I'm certain that if people work on this principle for half the time they squander, we will achieve permanent mindset and be able to perceive permanent Life. Let us believe that we can achieve it even sooner.

"Okay, but what if we don't succeed?" someone might object skeptically. The sophistication of this question tells me that they are completely capable of answering it on their own.

How would you live differently if you and your neighbor both live permanent lives? How would you mow the lawn tomorrow? Where would you select to build your compost pile? Would you still erect a fence full of innuendos?

How would the argument with your brother end if you face him forever? Would you be equally quick to hand-out or would you invest a moment of yourself to recognize there's a person involved? How differently would you plan for your elderly parents?

How about forgiveness? If you lived forever, would you unload and move on? Would you carry along grudges, hatred, and combat gear forever?

You need answers? Inquire within!

I trust you will find a "permanent" position somewhere inside. Maybe the child who was born expecting that Life is forever, that accountability is permanent, that others' rights to Life is eternal— still lives in you.

Perhaps we see even further now. By knowing our enemies will live forever, it's time to eliminate the conflict and carry on with one another.

"Nobody lives forever," you may argue. I have little rebuttal to that. However, think about a few social etiquettes that you simply will not violate. I would wager that none of them would harm anyone, yet you have learned to perceive them as unacceptable. We can condition ourselves to never look at life as temporary. The relative advantage is immeasurable.

In living permanently, we do indeed carry on forever. The only drawback is we might still die at 80, 95 or 110— but we'll leave behind the beginning to a permanent world.

Let us get permanent, lest the human struggle becomes permanent!

Don't be afraid your life will end;
be afraid that it will never begin.
— Grace Hansen

The Human Struggle

THE HUMAN STRUGGLE

*I trust you will find a "permanent" position some-
where inside. Maybe the child who was born expecting that Life is forever, that accountability is permanent, that others' rights to Life is eternal— still lives
in you.*

— The Paper Plate

Somewhere in a small town a woman is in love with a man from the city miles away. They both have reached firm conclusions about their religious belongings on their own. It happens that they share the same faith while enduring their own private struggles, and intimately involve God in each of their lives.

She confides in God about her weight problem, seeks *Their* guidance in working with the friction at her office, and prays for favorable results to the little things she does from day to day. She finds ways to see herself as an extension of God's work, even though the world and its cruelty tear her down, she says. Like others, she has dreams, which "seem to have gone up in smoke." She admits, "I've felt like I suddenly discovered the ground I was trying to stand on was really shifting sand."

She accepts and holds onto her life and the decisions she makes as the cards dealt by the only Hand. She wants to be an obedient follower and a trusting child. After all, she couldn't possibly question God's authority, or how *They* decide what is fair.

The man, meanwhile, seems to identify himself only with Christ and His work. This man has a very ill sister, for whom he feels great responsibilities, most of which he cannot attend to. He struggles with her illness and suffers immensely each of the times she tries to commit suicide. His sister would end up in lifeless comas for days while he would continually seek out his graceful God. Thus far, the resigned sister has recovered after each suicide attempt. He thanks God for *Their* unending grace, and she continues enduring life in sickness a few more days at a time.

While the man's faith endures, he struggles strangely though as his sister's miseries and suicidal episodes keep replaying time and again. It seems that God rewinds the clock for the man and his sister, but indifferently hangs it back on the same mural wall. The man submits to God almost helplessly that *They* lovingly will his life, then hangs on breathlessly until his sister gives in again. "Thy will be done…" he must believe in his mind.

How can people muster the motivation to live personal lives that are designed and commanded entirely by someone else, or by another being— albeit God?

We discussed in *The Paper Plate* that our perception is a precursor of thoughts, which in turn manage our perception and govern our expectations for Life and our behavior in Life. This seamless cycle also regulates people's interactions among one another, as well as within themselves. In addition, it can determine how successful we are in our relationships with God.

Perception and misunderstandings can plague many relationships. Remember when your parents thoroughly planned something with you in mind, but everything ended up as a disappointment because of some misunderstanding or failed expectations. You understand the seemingly insurmountable barrier that a parent-child relationship deals with at least some of the time.

Here's an example that shows how we've lived with inconsistent expectations for thousands of years. We know that most children manifest their best for their parents or relatives. If a child is the best she can be for her parents, can we reasonably expect her to be beyond human before God?

Suppose that child is you.

Perception and expectation can set up faulty premises that we must overcome. Our traditional expectations force us to forge different and disconnected lives. This disconnection, at fundamental levels, brings inconsistencies as we accumulate experiences over the course of many years, as do traditions over many generations. Perceptions and expectations can also establish a solid foundation that helps relationships last, but they must be consistent.

Knowing what to expect of ourselves is the first critical premise for building a relationship with God. To form a premise that passes the consistency test, is to expect ourselves to be the children that we realistically can be for God who knows the extent of our reach. We must not expect to be more than human with God, while accepting that we can be human with our parents.

Approach this one premise inconsistently, and we'll never achieve accord with *Them*. We are God's children whether we're sporting our Sunday attire or mid-week coveralls, whether we're carrying the cross or working the land. We must be the same children of Devine God, as we are of mortal parents.

It's time we think again about ourselves, lest the human pain and suffering should continue.

However, there are people who believe human sufferings are negligible, that we should be filled with humility and always walk humbly. They may remind us that Christ is the one who has made a serious sacrifice, or Buddha was the unselfish one, or Confucius who was the most thoughtful.

This belief is very evident in people who give their entire life for God. Perhaps they will discover one day that it isn't necessary; that God isn't who we perceive, understand, or expect. These devoted disciples might live entirely in solitude, in complete celibacy, or even in endless pain. God probably prefers that we live a life for ourselves and for one another, to improve humanity, and to truly reflect *Their* glory.

To avoid hardships, or to reduce the severity of pain, people learn from religion the practice of praising and praying to God. People pray to God for good health, lasting love, steady income, as well as salvation or afterlife. People then praise God for perceived answers to their prayers, and for gracious consideration of unanswered requests.

Why are our lives held together delicately by prayers?

We must ask for strength. We must ask for direction. We must beg for forgiveness. If we stand up on our own, that might be perceived as boastful, ungrateful, and disrespectful. It sounds like we must walk a religious tight rope— or we will be left fending for ourselves.

When no obvious answer to our prayers appears, people are left to wonder if it's a punishment. Then we must interpret for ourselves what the punishment is and for whatever wrong. We have no control after prayers leave our lips. We're taught to have faith that we will receive what we ask for somewhere in our lives. We're supposed to trust that it's helping us in ways we don't know or understand.

Is this a spiritual placebo?

People substitute key ingredients to having relationships with God by one hour each week before the altar, one Saturday or Sunday a week at Sabbath, or a couple of weeks of fasting each year, or whatever the religious regimen is. People murmur gracious praises to God, but count more on God's ability to know their displeasures within.

We tentatively live double lives, and utter with borrowed confidence that God has a plan. It's like trying to make sense of disappointments in your father by rationalizing with the little that you know of him, and giving him the benefit of the doubt. Isn't it demoralizing when all we have left is, "God has a plan"?

We're obviously not in the plan.

Can anyone really explain what's going on? What's this talk of the plan? Why do people insist on singing praises and chanting prayers amid unrelenting suffering, and continue this chatter about a plan?

Before we can understand what's going on between God and us, we must know God. Equally important is a premise upon which we perceive, interpret, and expect *Them.* Approach this second premise inconsistently, and we'll never achieve communion with *God.* We will understand this premise after we recognize that we've been estimating who God is, rather than seeking to understand *Them.*

When I ask God to help me win the lottery, I end up losing another dollar. I might think that God's not into gambling. When I pray for a loved one to never die, and find myself weeping over the irreversible loss, I might think that maybe God doesn't like favoritism. This estimation goes on, as we have been approximating God for thousands of years.

Our continuous reconstruction progressively reduces God to a commodity. God was in the beginning an almighty, all-being God. Then God was almighty, but not a gambling God and, later still, not a favoring God, and on we go. This progressive reconstruction eventually brings us to ask the question, "Can God create a rock so big that *They* can't carry it?"

God now must compete on the same market as Hulk Hogan and MTV, Bart Simpson and big screen movies, expensive diamonds and fast cars, science fiction and the paranormal.

It's time we think again about God, lest we keep on expecting a "plan," while we remain ignorant of our responsibilities.

To reconsider God's position and understand our place is to realize that while some people call it a plan, others call it destiny. The same people might say, "I don't believe in fate," and make claims about a plan in the same breath. Much of our pain comes from whether we perceive our lives as planned or written, or open to choice.

Are we living lives definitively drawn out by an engineer? Are we merely mice in a fixed maze, following confined walls along the way to inevitably end up at the finish? Winning a personal struggle would serve no purpose, for victory and defeat would be written. Whether it's a good or a bad plan, you will complete it. You will fulfill God's expectations.

Putting conscious effort into the plan would be extraneous, because we will be victorious by design, each according to our own program. People only need to point their finger at God, irrespective of the outcome. I don't see any point in anyone praying. Really, I doubt we can allow the notion of a pre-programmed life. If we accept that God created humankind with a purpose, having us live without consequence is not consistent.

If God doesn't draw out the plan to your life, do *They* wait at every turn deciding what's right and left for you? This premise presents some major confusion. For example, "Was that God telling me something, or just the little voices in my head?" Why does anyone bother making decisions, if a conductor keeps everything on track? We get away from a maze, only to end up on a track.

Not only are our lives not pre-programmed, they are not guided. Neither argument can stand the consistency test, which is the minimal requirement.

"God makes some decisions and you make some," some people may say. How do people decide which decisions they should make, and which decisions they should wait out? Look around you. Can you tell who have been warming the bench consequently? Once we sit out, it's difficult to know when we should engage again. Human partnerships can often work, but we are inadequate to be delegating our responsibility to God in any arrangement.

God doesn't play engineer, conductor, or arbitrator. Yet we have all lived at various times with one belief system then another, until we change systems in disillusion time and again.

In short, we must know who we are if we endeavor to have a relationship with God. We must also know who God is, or at least who God is not. Building upon the correct premises, perhaps we can adjust our perception and expectation of ourselves, of Life, and of God.

What we may expect also depends on how much responsibility we're willing to accept. We might have to do more than fulfill "God's calling," or believe that we're *Their* disposable instruments. People pray with the expectation that their prayers will be answered, yet wait for God to employ them.

We are useless really, you see— because a calling doesn't come to us unless we can contribute. By waiting around for a calling, we lack the readiness to make a difference.

We must remove our fixation with God's plan and how it might apply to us. We must think with confidence as we're endowed.

If God needs a doctor, does God particularly care if you're ready on your own initiative? If God needs a friend on earth to rescue a child lost searching for answers to her prayers, do *They* disqualify you for arriving on your own? While God might have a plan for me, I need to identify my plan, and fulfill it— to enlist myself as a prepared contributor. I'm standing by, and ready.

The instrumentation concept is very self-giving, but let's ask, "What kind of instrument am I?"

Am I a rock climber, skydiver, or professional student? Am I a Bible scholar, saint follower, or a disciple of immortal beings? Am I a trained eliminator who can pacify human conflicts by felling my own kind? Am I a politician pushing first-aid policies insensitive to extra-corporal constituents?

How about you, are you a scientist? Can God use you to repair the human rift? Are you an engineer, who God can use in a reconstruction? Are you a grower, carpenter, weaver, or counselor? Can God use you to fortify humanity? Are you, instead, the one God needs to subsidize?

If I am a procrastinator with little self-confidence and a learned fear for failures, where could I possibly fit in any of God's plans? While it is selfless that we give ourselves completely to God, be very aware, painfully if we must, what we're giving *Them*.

Even if we can decipher God's callings, or be worthy instruments to *Their* work, we must first understand our plans and bring them to fruition. As a good homemaker, perhaps God can put me in a family needing a strong mending fabric. As a good counselor, I might look to guide the perplexed. As refined instruments waiting for God's work, we will be seamlessly applied.

"Refined instruments" is the key, friends— not just blunt instruments.

When people find themselves ill equipped or poorly trained, they casually drag God into their troubles. "Oh God," they say, "We entrust our lives completely into your hands, as we are taught to do."

That's slick!

Pulling this quick one on God has several grave problems. We will discuss three of them: exploitation, despair, and doubt.

The first is a problem of convenience. People can tackle life head-on, but if things fail, they can say, "God didn't answer our prayers."

Particularly subtle is when we ask God to assist us in any fashion, we must have decided we won't or cannot accomplish it on our own. Is this a case of self-fulfilling prophecy, or is it a simpler case of self-doubt? Prophecy or doubt, it's counter-productive either way. Subconsciously, we might decide we don't want to make an effort in the first place. To have a better guarantee, people become accustomed to calling on the Magician.

This is exploitation.

By expecting God to stand by or assist us with our difficulties, we presume that others' troubles are lesser than our own. "If only I knew your infant was at home waiting for the milk, I wouldn't have taken the last carton." "If only I knew you had an emergency, I would have yielded the turning lane."

Some people believe God can help everybody simultaneously. We'll see in the remainder of this chapter, that the difference made to humanity does not rest in what God does, but in people's ability to see each other as equally important.

Moreover, by dragging God into our fights, however big or small, we cannot discern who is and who's not pulling the fair share of their weight. When things don't go our way is of great importance. I did my best; "I'm only human." By proclaiming to have done my best, is God then accused for not pulling *Their* share?

Be careful!

Let me summarize the first point by saying that we are not as humble as we aspire to be. We exploitatively use God as our "fall guy," while putting our needs before others'.

"Pulling this quick one on God" has another problem. When the Magician does not deliver, people call it a bad act. People often resign with "I can't understand," and regress with, "God must have a plan." People pray to sincerely include God in their struggles only to arrive at the dismal conclusion that God doesn't listen, doesn't care, or "we're not worth it."

Some day, we may even wonder if God really exists.

We have been asking, "God, hear our prayers," for *Them* to stop the human atrocities, and to fill ours hearts with love for one another. We even beg God to teach us to let go of our worries, and leave everything up to *Them*.

After several thousand years, people become accustomed to a sort of welfare program, if you will, and expound this arrogance that it's somehow our right to demand. "You're the one who put me on this earth." Hey, it's Your holy plan. So-called faith turns into reliance, skepticism, then quiet sarcasm and eventually name-calling— in disillusionment and despair.

The last of three serious problems we discuss here arise from our so-called "entrust" pretense. While people pull a blanket over God, their children convict them as hypocrites. People can manipulate and exploit yet call it entrusting. Meanwhile, we expect that our children have faith in us, but carry their own weight. "They need to be able to take care of themselves," we insist but, of course, we'll always be there for them. People obviously do not enjoy it when their own flesh and blood exploits them. We tend to disrespect ourselves. Our unwillingness to be simply obedient, without playing games, robs us of our ability to command our own children. This is disastrous because human progress depends on this ability to communicate and perpetuate a profound tradition.

Ask children if parents teach them that God helps those who help themselves. Ask them if they have seen or heard their parents whimpering to God before exhausting their human potential. Ask children if parents tend to rely on and abuse traditional practices and values, rather than protect them and improve them where appropriate. Sure, ask children if parents "entrust" not in faith but in selfish convenience. Ask them if they have problems with what parents believe versus what parents practice. Children will tell you, if you're prepared to hear what they say.

Deciding ahead of time, "you're not going to make it" is self-defeating. Calling upon God as an added personal guarantee is selfish. Not being able to educate our own children without a dance is futile, for they are the connecting pieces to the future of humanity.

Examining the three issues we discussed, exploitation, despair, and doubt, one surprising commonality emerges; we include God in our struggles. The answer to our seemingly endless trials is simple, really, and would make conventional wisdom very uncomfortable.

Do not include God in our struggles!

Instead, we must know that God instilled in us the power to rise above human tribulations.

The problems we encounter are in themselves "human." We have the faculties to deal with them. We must develop and apply these faculties, lest our complacency distorts the relative magnitude of our hardships. When we stand still or digress, our troubles can appear to outpace our capacities to accept, understand, and manage.

If an extra-human problem were before us, we cannot know of it. When an event is beyond our perceptive capability, we cannot be cognizant of it. Give a five-year-old your income tax, and you'll see what I mean.

Can we perceive God-problems?

Be careful.

The promised kingdom belongs to us, but God made it accessible only by a mature human race. To safeguard the kingdom from ill intentions, evil wanderers, and intruders, God made the entrance to the kingdom a challenge— surmountable only by refined humankind.

We must realize that God endowed the human race with the most incredible tool— the ability to understand more tomorrow than we do today, to know more later than we know now, and to grow closer to God each time we triumph. With each step on the permanent journey, we come closer to obtaining the key to the Promised Land.

"Do not include God in our struggles!" While sharply contrary to conventional wisdom, this principle guarantees that we apply and advance ourselves. God cannot compromise and expose this sacred kingdom to those who cannot manage it.

Instead, *They* completely trust that we will discover the kingdom using our own "instruments."

Until people are 16 years old, they cannot have the key to a car. Until officials are inducted, they cannot govern. Until humankind reaches spiritual maturity, they cannot access the Garden of Eden.

Poignantly, this is why many prayers don't appear to be answered. We ask for "keys" big and small, while oblivious to the fact that we need maturity from personally taking the permanent journey to manage the key, secure the entrance to the kingdom, understand, and protect the kingdom.

Inherently, goodness must be more intelligent and more resilient than evil; goodness must be more responsible and more thoughtful than evil. From *The Dogma*: "We must understand that God does not share the other side of the coin with the devil, as our casual language and religious cultures suggest. This is not a 50-50 toss— but an eventual and certain eclipse by God and *Their* creations."

Consistent with our inborn potential, God expects us to eventually mature beyond spiritual adolescence— and become custodians of the garden of old.

*The only ZEN you find on the tops of mountains
is the ZEN you bring up there.*
— Robert M. Pirsig

The Image

THE IMAGE

"We must understand that God does not share the other side of the coin with the devil, as our casual language and religious cultures suggest. This is not a 50-50 toss— but an eventual and certain eclipse by God and Their *creations."*

— *The Human Struggle*

You know, "the yolk of Life is carried and delivered by the bearer, or woman, as we have seen consistently. We may insist that God is more than both man and woman, but certainly not only man. While the use of human pronouns cannot change the nature of Almighty God, we need to be consistent so we can prevail."[1]

God is one entity, but not depictable in singular form.

Although humans are marvelous wonders with the most endowed brains, language is our only knowledge exchange tool. One way or another, we have to pictorially transcribe our thoughts before we can convey them. People rely on pictures and graphs, signs and symbols, which for the most part comprise the human language.

---

[1] Taken from *The Beginning*.

I have to write a letter to tell how I feel. If I want to teach science, I have to draw simplified illustrations. Granted, people do not draw pictures or pictograms in everyday use, but that's because we memorize them.

Unlike other weaknesses that people can conceal, it's obvious that language is our only tool for communication. If someone could interfere with our systems of symbols, we would be "at a loss for words." If an evil tyrant wanted to hinder or destroy us, language would become a futile battleground for humanity.

While language is our only communication mechanism, we can surpass this limitation by having our thoughts transcend language. This is possible because thoughts cannot be constrained by graphs or pictograms. Creative thinking is the only human ability that is unlimited, by the nature of our endowment.

We may communicate as far as language takes us— but we must think beyond what we're able to articulate.

The issue is that, over time, language has become the bubble for our communication. This language bubble regulates how people speak and write, as well as how people receive and interpret messages. Incoming and outgoing information are limited to what we have inside this bubble. Information is gibberish, otherwise, if we can't translate it somehow.

People now confine thoughts inside this bubble, too, and become comfortable thinking via language. This mode of thinking is a simple matter of practicality, really. For instance, people cannot think of colors beyond those they can actually write down or tell someone about. It's been practical because, for the most part, we haven't had a need for that *off-color* language anyhow. Now though, the issue at hand is larger than Life or, at least, much larger than language.

Must human's communicative capacity stop at English, Greek, or Chinese; sign language, body gestures, or some other prescribed convention? The human thinking machine must be more than a vocabulary manipulating apparatus.

To "burst your bubble" is to use language to feed thoughts, but not thoughts merely as a resultant component of language. Understand that our thinking machine produces thoughts, while language only delivers and receives them. We must stop this confusion, because humanity needs to move on.

A necessary relationship exists between the thinking machine and the language bubble, because they require the same big-brain. As long as we cannot think outside the bubble, language subsequently stands still. In turn, the bubble, which now confines thoughts, remains in regress. Granted human languages have changed slowly over the millennia, they have not been a result of progressive thoughts. Rather, this change has been mostly due to the coining of "tangible" finds, be they scientific or theological.

As a result, we cannot think of God outside of the bubble, because language says— "That has not been defined."

Perhaps, one day, we will have an alternate method of knowledge transfer. Until then, we have no choice but to force language to perform in ways it doesn't want to, or is incapable of doing. I ask that we all participate in taking the leap that words customarily fail on paper, so we can elevate our minds and attain the required threshold perspective to know God.

People have debated about who God is and what *They* look like, since the beginning of time. For Christians, there was Christ, who they could draw and satisfy their needs to visually connect with God. Buddhists have the icon Buddha in every aspect of their life, even though Buddha isn't their god. Other religions have their own ideas of who God is, too, and how to be closer to *Them*.

Is God everywhere? Does God really know everything? How angry can *They* get? Can God create a rock so big *They* can't carry it?

Here's a question people forget to ask: Are we willing to worship an almighty-minus-one god, who the *Parents* don't recognize?

I am not qualified to judge who you proclaim as God. I will not convince you that my God is the God for you. I will not tell you where you'll end up, if you don't believe in what I believe. I will say that because of the consistency requirement, there must be one, and only one, Almighty God. There is no need to describe or distinguish which god is yours or mine, when there is but one God.

If you believe in God, the Creator, or our *Parents*, and want to see *Them* vividly in your mind and feel *Their* burning fire in your life, you must think outside of the bubble.

The first bubble that we must break is the notion that each faith can have its own almighty god of the universe. As long as we discuss an "Almighty" God, there must be only one.

Suppose you and I are the only people in the whole world. We each live on our own continent, and have no knowledge of the other's existence. Never mind, for the moment, what you and I believe, how we each hunt, care for our family, or to whom we pray at night.

One day, we meet each other in passing; what a surprise, of course. I cautiously approach you, and you watchfully examine me. We can visibly see that we don't look or sound exactly alike. While different, we can recognize each other's hands, feet, and face, noticing the different hair colors, skin textures, and where we carry our winter reserves. We find these differences interesting, but they do not alarm us, as if we each know that they simply allow us to be different.

More intriguing are our similarities, as we gaze at one another. We perceive each other as a unique being with individual physical characteristics. Subtly inside, we share a warm feeling that we now belong— in friendship and in each other. There is a connection unlike what we find with plants, animals, and other living things. While some people may argue that they connect permanently with nature, the power in human connections remains the most vital.

If your Creator lives in you, and we belong in each other, it's precipitous that your Creator is none other than mine.

On the other hand, you may claim that you do not have a Creator, while I do and that *They* live in me. Because we belong in each other, my Creator is none other than yours.

You may insist that we do not belong in one another, and you're certain that you feel no connection. In that case, you are not ready to leave the bubble.

Accept our common origin, or we both risk damaging the relationship we long for with our God, who, unbeknown to us, is the same One.

Who is this God?

It's widely accepted that God created us in *Their* image— not physical, emotional, or spiritual image— but *Their* image. Many people insist that we were created physically like God, and in the same breath maintain that God is not physical. We were created like God! Another 6,000 years will not lessen the pain of our indecision.

Doesn't that blanket you with powerful emotions? We were created like God. Without having a Bible study over our likeness, let's think about what this means.

You and I being like *Them* means that God, too, is like us.

You ought to feel the power!

What if the Creator you believe in isn't in the Torah, Koran, or Bible? Perhaps your entire faith isn't even built on a book. No such pivotal record that your Creator indeed created you in *Their* image. Is there a different chapter for you?

Understand that because we come from one Creator, the boundaries of our belonging or membership aren't divisible by books; but only by the ability of our minds.

The answer to the no-book dilemma lies in the simple fact that, while not recorded as supposed, your Creator is almighty and all-being. That prevailing truth doesn't even have to be recorded. If your God is all things, it must follow that anything *They* create is a subset of "all things"— like *Them* and in *Them*, although in varying degrees. Thus, whether recorded that you were created in the likeness of your Creator, you inescapably are in *Their* image.

Let's celebrate with some good old memories.

Remember the innocent days of black–and-white home movies on reels? You had to have a movie projector, a white screen of some sort, and a bucket of film. Remember how we could move the projector to the back of the room by dragging the flimsy table it sat on. As we did that, the image on the screen would get larger, and we would have to tweak the focus adjustments. We didn't want to drag the projector too far back, or the image would spill off the screen. Well, we need that old projector again.

Suppose you and I are each made up of two features. I am short and sweet, and you're tall and handsome. I take my features, put them into the film bucket, and turn on the projector. Looking at the screen, I am fairly pleased. It's me. You decline to do the same, because you don't enjoy looking at yourself.

However, you are okay with putting your features into the bucket as long as mine are in there as well.

Then we show the picture on the screen. Sure enough, it's you and me, all right, after a quick mental sort. After all, there are only four features to really sort out, so it doesn't take the brain too long.

We crank it up and add to the film bucket that I am intelligent and studious, while you are quick, wise, and forgiving. The projected image of the two of us seems boxy and jagged. Additionally, I like motorcycling, computers, writing, boats, and cars; you enjoy sailing, charity work, writing, and fishing, as well as diving. We're starting to get some depth to the picture.

I can admit that I can have a temper, could probably hurt someone, but am normally compassionate. You, on the other hand, become excited easily, tend to ignore people of the opposite sex, love animals, and are prone to not pay back personal loans. We take these features and toss them all into the film bucket. One last check with the projector shows that it's a better and more realistic representation of you and me. Cool.

Then we throw everything about you and me into bucket, until the projector shows only a larger picture of ourselves. We can see the different scars we each have on our knees, as well as the way the hair strands on our head reflect light. In addition to the exact physical features, we can see in your and my faces the personal expressions, and we immediately recognize them as our own.

While physical, our individual postures also say much about our attitudes about life and toward each other. The image is so real and life like now. Wow! We both especially like the fact that we appear bigger on screen. When looking at ourselves individually, we see that I fit the profile of a short, sweet, intelligent, and studious person, who likes motorcycling, computers, writing, boats and, cars, who can succumb to anger, yet compassionate.

My descriptors together make up my essence, if you will, and your descriptors make up your essence. Together, on the big screen, my essence and yours interact, producing yet a third image, the image that your and my minds really see.

We both enjoy the third image immensely, and call it friendship.

After looking at the screen, we're fairly amazed that something like that could come from a mixed bag of individual features or descriptions. A short while later, we seem to all but ignore the reflection on the hair, or the one arm strapping across the other's shoulders. We find the whole picture more multifaceted, more balanced, more capable, and somehow more important than your or my image alone. Out of the third image, we subsequently find the third essence, or the essence of friendship.

So, we set out to find more essences, as a personal challenge, to build a friendship big enough to fill the entire room. Over time, the bucket becomes laden with all of the essences that we gather around the entire world. We collect from Buddhists, atheists, Christians, Jews, engineers, homemakers, doctors, beggars, and everyone, whether they practice any religion. We collect from politicians, historians, judges, and lawmakers. We even include grandparents, parents, husbands, wives, and their children.

For good or for bad, there are multitudes of essences in this world. We become burdened and saddened, for we find in our bucket ugly traces of humanity, too; the essence of murderers, sex offenders, political terrorists, and the horrors, the crying of pain, the killing and dying. We simply realize that we are not going to leave out anyone.

Our film bucket is now filled to the top with every essence of everyone, everywhere. In addition, there seems to be dynamic reactions among them, where their interactions produce additional essences in some cases. In other cases, the interactions seem to overwhelm some other essences in the mix and nullify them.

We hurry back to the media room with our heavy bucket, and project everything on the screen. Oddly, we can no longer distinguish an image. We fuss with the focus adjustments, but can't improve the picture. There must be too much in the film, as we have never tried to project anything like this before. We attempt to improve the picture, as we have done many times past, by moving the projector further away, but strangely find no improvement.

It looks as if the image is much too thick right out of the projector. We persist by moving the projector still farther back, and keep on going until we begin to see something on the screen.

Before we notice it, we have backed ourselves right out of the back wall, and the image now casts itself over the entire room. We still need a better image, so we move an incredible distance away from our original place. We keep going as the image slowly clears. While it gradually focuses, the image also grows larger and larger, as we back up more and more. Suddenly, we can no longer return to the same place from where we started.

We're in the middle of absolutely nothing now, in some blackness of empty space with only the projector. The image we try to view, meanwhile, seems like light-years away since we last saw it; no room, no walls, no ordinary white screen anywhere.

As the image progressively clears up, we're astonished by the staggering size that it has become. The original portable screen, which we relied on earlier, is now less than half a tight stitch on the new screen. Immeasurable!

The image is beyond galactic dimensions. Even though it appears to be some remote distance away, there is a touchable liveliness to it. If we look hard enough, we can almost see the interactions of so much essence, teaming continuously just under the canvass.

Suddenly, a deafening roar of acclamation booms across the silent domain. We look up to see the image on the inter-galactic screen— is that of our *Parents*.

By creating us all in *Their* image, God gave us the key to *Their* presence. This discovery is a monumental instrument of tremendous importance and power. This means that when we come together in essence, we can embrace God personally and directly without intermediary deities, interceding prayers, or pointless human theatricals.

Do I see a deep puzzling brow on your face? You are un-comfortable accepting God's image, which shares essences with killers, rapists, molesters, and the back stabbers of the world. You and I admit that we collected everyone earlier, be-cause we wanted to project the largest image of friendship.

How can we say that God possesses human characteris-tics that are worthy only of evening news? How can God fit in a local criminal lineup? We feel like hell is going to find us, simply for thinking that God shares the mind with terrorists and felons.

Your trouble, my friends, is human. Nonetheless, we bear the responsibility to recognize that which is of our essence, and that which is beyond us. To understand this is to realize that a human characteristic, say murderous, turns a person into some-one who kills unjustly or unfairly. In God, however, such a characteristic does not produce a murderous God, because *They* command each and all essences by *Their* will.

God must encompass all good essences, as well as all that is evil. Rest assured it would take a God trait to turn God one way or another, while it merely takes a human trait to change you and me. How is it that people keep talking about being humble, and at the same time believe in a notion that humans have the potency to infect God?

A single human being is a miniature subset of God, one single frame from the film. The murderer among us represents a dark frame, or a pathological imbalance of the human condition. If we extract another frame from the film, we might see a different miniature with a different set of tendencies, suppose, to anger or a propensity to hurt. The human murderer in God is neutralized by *Their* comprehensive complementary essences.

This is the fundamental understanding that we have been lacking to comprehend the power of God's being. We have been refusing to see *Them* in the same mirror that we see ourselves. Because we are in *Their* image, God is positively the collection of ours.

People customarily discard the idea that God could be anything like us, as we are imperfect and visibly lacking any God-like feature. God is not a thief. God is not a liar, a procrastinator, a loser, or a name caller.

You see, people are conditioned to see themselves as worthless and dispensable soldiers of an instituted religion regimented by dogma. Many people have become accustomed, over the millennia, to the idea that we are foremost sinners.

Oh sure, "We merely look like God." At the same time, some people say that God is much more than physical. Do we look like *Them* only when *They* materialize in the flesh?

We must accept that whatever children we have become, there's no changing the fact that we belong to our *Parents.* Some people might be damned criminals, but their heritage is still from God. When we stop thinking about God in terms of you and me, individually, we will be able to reflect instead on human wholeness, or complete assembly.

Where is our humbleness, as we conceit that God can be seen merely by looking at humankind?

It's obvious! The real humbleness is in the realization of what a fraction of God we each are.

This humbleness is the willingness to pick up the slack before us and to tighten community ties. This humbleness lies in our accepting that it takes all of us to project the Almighty Image. Just a holy man won't do; just a martyr won't do; I can't, nor can you— alone.

Humbleness is not useful as any form of denial.

We were created in God's image.

God remains straight and true because *They* are the sole holder of the complete deck, to put it differently. By duplicating us in *Them*, there is now a mirrored deck to be assembled in humanity.

There are two copies of the same print, the Original and a duplicate set. The delicacy of this second set lies in its many exposures, as in the Original, in addition to the fact that each exposure must assemble on its individual will. Unlike a jigsaw puzzle, no one can put us together.

That is why our *Parents* don't force us to unite, although *They* trust that we do. That, too, is why God does not coerce repentance or salvation onto us.

Until the odds of assembling are overcome, the duplicate set will remain incoherent. We can assemble the code and unlock the magic in the "mirrored deck," or we can wait out for the unscheduled return of the Original.

There are reasons to believe that God will return after all people have found peace. What do you suppose that means? Is it possible that after we have found peace, the individual images of God will come together in our assembly— hence God's return in us?

Then, where should we be looking for *Them*? Where can we find answers to our prayers?

Recall that we posed some questions earlier in this chapter. Is God everywhere? Does God really know everything? How angry can God get? I trust you realize now, that the answers to these questions lie in all of us.

We can now envision God as never before. We appreciate that obedience to the second commandment is finally possible. For Judeo-Christian traditions, it is to make no graven image of God. People dangle these graven images in their automobiles, hang them all over their houses, and go about with them in their pockets. Who do you think people have been worshiping or idolizing, if these are nowhere near the images of God?

To make a graven image of God, now, means to depict the entire human race in assembly or unity. This is not as simple as the portraits we paint, or the assortments of objects we currently have of God. It is natural that the second commandment is observed.

The only image of God we will make from now on is in our assembly one day.

This is not a new idea, but I trust it makes sense now.

Look at the images.

Does God really know everything? What is everything anyway? Is it all [human] knowledge combined from past, present, and future?

Who's asking the question?

If God knows more than what we know, *Their* knowledge would be outside of our cognitive capability. We could not account for it. Whether God knows everything would not matter in this case, if we have no benchmark or notion of God's knowledge.

The human questions are perplexing, really, but that's because people don't know what they're asking. The question perhaps should be re-phrased to ask, does God know more than the collective humans do?

Because we have not been able to melt our knowledge together at will lately, it seems that this newer question is also beyond us.

Does God know about everything in the whole universe? Let me answer your question this way. Is this a challenge, or are you still trying to determine whether you have the right god?

Look at the images.

People have long wondered, "How angry can God get?" What are they asking, do they know? Anger is a human trait or essence, if you will. It's from our lack of strength that we slam our fist on the table. It's out of greed for power that we oppress the weak. It's from fear that we terrorize. Anger is another case of human pathology.

There are also countless other questions about God. One troubling question stands out— "Can God create a rock so big that *They* can't carry it?"

This is troubling because, in the form of a question, it provides a perplexed glimpse into the human struggle. That is, people find it necessary to re-ascertain the reasons they believe in God, or they're merely comparison-shopping for reasons to believe still.

Let me ask a simpler question. Can you stuff a bag so big that you can't haul it?

The real power is not in the "can" concept.

The debate is that if God is almighty, then *They* must be able to create the ultimate rock. The same person struggles with the human humor that if God put *Themselves* under a rock that *They* can't carry, then *They* are not almighty. On the other hand, suppose God can carry the rock, then the rock *They* create isn't the ultimate.

Well, can you stuff a bag so big that you cannot haul it?

There is a serious issue weighing just as much as the rock. Who are we to imply that God's decisions and actions are based on might? Who are we to insist that physical might is *Their* highest power?

People need to understand what they mean when they use language in the bubble. Are we talking about Hercules when we say almighty, a gazillion Hercules, or do we mean the absolute harmony of all God-essences?

Having said that, can God create a rock so big *They* can't carry it?

If you're still looking for an answer— you're asking the wrong question.

On the other hand, if we genuinely seek to know and understand God, we must realize that the more essence we retrieve, the more we directly know ourselves. From our big screen projector, it follows— the better we, too, know God.

Which essences of yourself did you hold back earlier? Which essences of yourself did you not know of then? Which essences of one another did we ignore?

Let us define ourselves, refine humanity, and assemble the fragments of God.

The nature of God is a circle of which the center is
everywhere
and the circumference is
nowhere.
— Empedocles

The Essence

THE ESSENCE

"God remains straight and true because They *are the sole holder of the complete deck, to put it differently. By duplicating us in* Them, *there is now a mirrored deck to be assembled in humanity."*

—*The Image*

Ahuman baby is completely powerless at birth, and can perish without the care of its parents. Like God, with *Their* all-around power who cannot err, a child with her complete lack of power, can do no wrong. A child is conceived by the design of God, the giving act of two human parents, and the joining of their essences.

The child in you and me grows, and incrementally attains the ability to coo and crawl, to concentrate and follow, to talk and think some time later. We soon achieve cognition and the power to move ourselves, as well as others eventually in life.

Oddly, we can now err and do so often.

As we continue to grow, doctrines imperceptibly embed in us the first virtue— selflessness, or self-denial. In one form or another, self-denial is the ultimate power we're taught to perceive. Many people confuse this self-denial for self-control, which is a powerful virtue. While it is a power no one other than the self might attain, self-control does not have to be self-denial.

It would be more inspiring if people fulfill themselves to the fullest, just short of depriving one another.

That's control. That— is power.

Many people later learn, from institutionalized religions, that self-denial brings them a heavenly body.

Without knowledge, self-denial is mistaken for self-control. Without understanding, self-deprivation is mistaken for victories over our desires. Instead of managing our enjoyment for alcohol, some people force themselves to quit drinking it altogether. Instead of arbitrating with neighbors and friends when there's a conflict, our tendency is to avoid them. Rather than controlling the *selves* in us, many people suppress these selves for as long as a lifetime.

Deprivation, ironically, gives rise to temptations.

Many people don't fulfill themselves. They indulge.

While very powerful after they've grown, people are now relatively corrupt in their fight for so-called self-control and self-indulgence.

Eventually, most people can no longer see their own essence or the reasons they exist. As they get older, and are laden with responsibilities, many people begin to rely on tradition, teachings, and religious dogma to tell them what and who they are. Self-doubt, denial, greed, hate, and envy progressively shadow self-image, until people can no longer find themselves in one another.

The answer to this dilemma of self-identity and intimacy rests, once again, within us.

To understand ourselves, we need to first find meanings to our mental, physical, psychological, spiritual, and emotional *selves* in the individuals that we each are. Recall from *The Beginning,* "Whether we ever could see our whole beings before, we had become most visibly physical, mental, emotional, psychological, and spiritual beings. It's as if we were each, in ourselves, one individual but no longer singular— like God in a way."

What are our essences? In what ways are we supposed to affect Life, or what role are we to play in the maturing of the human race? We need the answer to this question not only to know ourselves but, also, to directly know God.

What are we made of, what are we good with, and where are we going with our essence?

Ask your parents, "How soon after birth did I first recognize myself in the mirror, and call out my name?"

How long do you take to see yourself now?

Do you avoid looking at yourself in the mirror? How about seeing yourself in photographs? Photos and mirrors reveal people's physical essences, for the most part. Rather than being intimate with them, many of us find them intriguing, to put it nicely. For the vast majority of people, these images reveal the *selves* to which we don't immediately relate, at least not entirely.

If the images of God are in us, and we are uncomfortable looking at ourselves— how do we relate to *Them*?

Though small, this is a powerful indication that we need this exercise in human essence. It follows that a search for essence must begin.

Ask your parents, "In what essence was I conceived?"

Beginning with your time in the womb, until the day you first took cognitive control of your being, what became a part of you? We need to focus on the main objective, which is to find and define our essences, reinforce and enrich them. We need to stay clear of the preoccupation with dates and times of our first encounters with the mirror, the self, or other chronological specifics.

For instance, I was conceived in lust, hope, self-fulfillment, dreams, strength, and the perceived responsibility to procreate. My parents were both *lustful* with each other in their passion, and they *hoped* that they would produce a child, to begin the *fulfillment* of a new family. My parents shared a common feeling of *strength* when they were together, a strength they knew would be required to raise a *strong* child.

I was also conceived in *longing,* as my father always wanted my mother at his side. My mother always wanted to give, and thus one of my essences is *giving*, to fulfill external as well as internal needs. More than these attributes, I was conceived in *pride* with the essence of *trust*, as my father was a very *confident* man and my mother was all-trusting in her husband. My parents also had *aspirations* of the prevalent *good* rising, and forever keeping bad at bay.

There is more than meets the eye, of course. Perhaps I was also conceived in *impatience*, for the time of war was wearing the people thin; in *resentment* that there was so much dying and hurting; in *believing* that hardships would eventually pass. There were accusations and blames in my mother's family for her disobedience in marrying my father. Maybe I was conceived in desire for *belonging, acceptance*, and *forgiveness* as a result.

These are my essences. For me to know me is to find intimacy in my essences and nurture each essence to its fullest.

As it is with any new goal, we must often do things we have not done before. In this case, learning about something we have never known is to take a courageous step in a new direction.

Ask your parents, "In what essence was I conceived?"

This is a new monumental step in human communication, as you will discover, if you haven't already. You might need to give your parents a chance to prepare their responses ahead of time, but they will tell you. Many of our parents are not good communicators or willing listeners, so we need to approach them tactfully about this subject.

You are still the single most indispensable player in discovering your own essences. Your parents can fill in the many years before you acquired your thinking ability and cognitive awareness of yourself. Your parents hold the information about your earlier years, which are profound to your development later in life. Some of what they share with you about yourself may upset you, but perhaps these are essences with the most potential.

Like a weak point in the bone that breaks and heals twice as strong, an essence recognized as your shortcoming can be leveraged to compliment you. Until you have an opportunity to discover who you are, you could be beating yourself up only for sympathy. Worse, you could be pumping and touting essences you believe are yours.

Agreeable findings reinforce what you have believed and established about yourself. They offer you a specific apparatus to help nourish and fortify your less favorable essences.

For example, suppose anger and hate are my "less favorable essences," which can ignite quickly and ferociously. This ignition usually launches me into some feverish determination. Determination has a positive influence for the most part unless, of course, the determination is revenge to injure or to kill.

Like fire fighters who start fires to contain fires— I too can contemplate my anger and head it off. This is possible only by knowing, intimately, that I can get angry and lay out approaches in case the trigger events transpire. For the most part, we all do this already to some extent except by avoidance, rather than by resolution.

Ask yourself: What can trigger my anger? Do these triggers work all the time, or do they depend on certain circumstances?

This is intimate self-imaging.

It follows that merely avoiding the end result, or anger in this case, often doesn't work because we can't successfully avoid life much of the time. The work invested to achieve this intimacy is far more beneficial than playing avoidance's wheel of chance all of our lives.

In the natural world, we have essences that can be much worse than anger and hate. They can be prejudice, cruelty, and greed in varying severity. They, too, make up the individuals that we are. The human imperfections remind us of the divine separation between humankind and God. That is, we are imbalanced.

The more intimate we are with our essences, the better we can counteract and even compliment them, rather than merely reacting to them.

Additionally, we need to learn about our human conception from human observers. Do not enlist God's help, because *They*'re the ultimate subject of our endeavor. If we enlist God's help, we violate the resolution drafted in *The Human Struggle*. Many people insist on asking God directly or worse yet, they ask, "God, please take my life in your hands," I would like to be carried instead.

If our purpose is to understand ourselves so that we may understand God, we don't yet know God. More critically, we don't know how to commune with *Them*. By asking God the questions directly and prematurely, we chance not comprehending *Their* answers and misread *Their* intent. Because we don't do our homework, we misunderstand, which causes anger and hate to fester within.

As natural as human languages are, we all must learn them if we want to understand and be understood. Yet, we want a quick fix when forming a relationship with God, and we try to converse with *Them* prematurely. How do we expect to utter gibberish to our *Parents*, and have a gainful conversation?

Engaging God prematurely leaves out fundamental building blocks of mutual communion. We build one-way expectations, and disillusion ourselves with misunderstandings. This kind of simplification produces a paradox from which we have entrapped ourselves. This has resulted in witch-hunting for much too long.

When we talk to God before we're ready, we consequently think we hear responses that we cannot identify, or suggestions that we cannot discern. We tend to fill in the blanks and, ultimately, are not satisfied.

People unknowingly suffer a dismal future while they miss out on the present. A future based on language that becomes increasingly foreign with each passing day. To understand this, we only need to recall a family dinner or breakfast scene where there's at least one parent and one teenage child present.

You see, Spanish or Chinese could be the language that the parent and the teenager share, but they do not communicate very well. The Chinese teen might not talk back as much, and the Latino parent might not be as stern, but the disconnection is surely present across both tables. Like our communion with God, the teen improvises to meet an obligation, rather than learning to build a relationship on communion. The language becomes more foreign at dinner over the years, just like our future becomes more obscure with God.

A dangerous table is set. We now have a resentful child, and the *Parents* who appear to be absent.

Have you heard, "God can read our minds"?

Tragically— we cannot read *Theirs*.

Hastening our communication with God is disastrous, as human history can attest. We must complete our mission of self-imaging, for we owe God at least a proper and thorough introduction of ourselves.

I cannot stress enough about self-imaging. You will not even scare the devil if you don't know who you are. You cannot introduce yourself to your *Parents* or be *Their* instrument, if you merely know that "I'm only human."

Perhaps, you actually have the answers to your conception and upbringing, and understand who you have become. Are these answers in alignment with who you aspire to be? Do you mentally align with them, or just habitually? Can you come to terms with all of them?

You might have ideals higher than those in which you were conceived. You might be more romantic than your parents were. Perhaps you have managed to detach yourself from the physical lust in their marriage.

You may have essences you believe helped conceive you, but you can't carry it out. If that's the case, it's time you disconnect from them. When you know and understand your essences, conceived or acquired, you can eliminate the ones that don't fit you, and nourish the ones that help you grow.

Consequently, Life as we know it begins with each of our individual *selves*. I cannot understand anyone else if I cannot figure out myself. I can't "love my neighbors as myself," if I don't like myself. How do I begin to understand you when I don't entirely understand me?

Knowing the essences in which you were conceived, you can work out the essences of you now. Remember, we must nourish and nurture these essences to fulfillment. By doing this, we will become intimate with ourselves as we arrive intimately at our total essence. Only then can we begin to love ourselves— and eventually one another.

Nature doesn't do something before its time. Nature does not resist anything when it is time. We, too, will love each other naturally— once we learn how to love our individual *selves*.

As trivial as it may sound, a tougher heart to win over is not your neighbor's, but your own. A harder plight to beat is not hunger, but personal doubt. A better gift is not something expensive, but the value you share. Making all socially and politically correct gestures are only rehearsals for the act of love we have yet to perfect.

One final obstacle between humans and God is our insistence on humbleness and humility.

Many people believe that, due to our unworthiness, we must get to the Almighty Creator through a qualified intermediary being. For example, many Christians believe they must come to God through Jesus. That seems like a humble thing to do, but it's filled with problems and inconsistencies.

Jesus was a time-specific manifestation of God. People have long squandered that time. If we want to live in the Light, do so; if we want to live by forgiving others, do so; if we want to live in tolerance, acceptance, and trust— do so.

Live in God!

As Jesus defied death on the third day, he transformed in his ascension— he was Jesus no more! Jesus returned to heaven as God.

God!

Jesus left the human world. *He* left the language bubble. If we believed in Jesus, we have the obligation to believe in God.

I realize the vast majority of Christians are faithful followers of Jesus Christ. If you must be humble, and commune with God through the ascended Jesus, fine— but do just what you declare.

First, you better start out by finding *Him*. He is not suspended on the cross. He is not framed in the human face on the wall. Most critically, *He* is not the messaging service. You want to find *Him*?

God's throne is where *He* is!

The middleman, as we like to think, is only there in human fixation. It's like a looping hologram in the big brain. You see, the flat mind failed to transform the image of Jesus as *He* left the ground people stood on.

If people must have an ornament on the altar or a pendant hanging from their rear-view mirror, do embody Jesus in anything but death. Why not choose a bud of flower. Put a bud on the altar, hang a bud on your wall, and proclaim that this is the Bud of Life.

Some people wonder why their prayers aren't heard. Have they been addressing the correct recipient?

If your faith doesn't include Jesus, who do you use as an intermediary deity? Are your prayers answered?

One hint: "We have a plan," is not likely an answer from God.

People make a virtue out of humbleness, but they haven't really pondered what it means. To be humble before others means that we must rank among them, yet we choose to lower our pride and be modest and unassuming.

What am I getting at? Suppose you did very well in school the last semester and were recognized for your achievements. You received many congratulations and were a likely envy of the school, but were probably a bit embarrassed.

While knowing you earned the accolades, you were uncomfortable beating your own chest as you suspect some others might have had a more impressive climb. You're probably more inclined to attribute your success to your friends and parents, and to quietly thank God for the outcome. You realize, too, that you might be tested again; so you prepare yourself with confidence, and quietly accept to once again rank among peers.

People do not rank anywhere with God.

We are not God's classmates, colleagues, or even foes. You and I seem to have agreed long ago that we are at the bottom of *Their* ladder. To say that we yield, lower, or look to the ground is inconsistent. We are at ground level! We do not possess any latitude to yield. We do not have any height to lower.

With respect to God, we are in no position to "lower our pride and be modest and unassuming."

Humbleness among peers is human.

Humbleness before God is foolish.

Perhaps it will be more apparent where we stand, when we really know who we are.

> *The perfect human being is*
> *all human beings put together,*
> *it is a collective,*
> *it is all of us together that make perfection.*
> — Socrates

The Hope

THE HOPE

One time, my four-year-old son, Max, wondered what hope meant. His mom turned the question back to him, "What do you think it means?" He thought for a moment then said, "It means you're afraid of something."

— Max Tran

Recall, in the latter part of *The Human Struggle*, that we realized true relationships with God shouldn't be enduring. I described how we could confidently live in Life by knowing the key to the human struggles. This key consists of a commitment not to include God in our struggles, along with the knowledge that God will protect humankind's chances of claiming the kingdom by not compromising privileged information.

Without this commitment and knowledge, people can only hope.

More than prayers and formal enlistments of God, hope opens *The Human Struggle's* exploitation to people as well. Hope is, by nature, an indirect form of solicitation, not unlike asking and expecting in formal prayers.

When I hope that you come to visit, I place some burden on you. I'm effectively enlisting or calling on you. In response, you must think about my invitation and weigh it out with other competing factors in your life. I can hope for things, which can put quite a load on you, whether you choose to oblige. Similarly, anyone can put these types of burdens on anyone else.

People can, and do, hope for things from God. With God though, people are more presumptuous, for they might not ask explicitly. It's as if I just hope inside my of head, while relying on God to synchronize with my thoughts.

Not only does hope have great latitude, it has its own institution. In one representation or another, it's the institution of charity. People call it many different things, but charity is the primary function.

Have we an entire establishment designed to bandage people?

Don't get me wrong. Helping others under any name or circumstance is, in itself, a powerful virtue. I must question whether hope really helps.

Hope is a powerful motivator, yet it doesn't deter suffering from inflicting on both strong and weak people. Hope can be persistent, but it cannot make fortunate events more likely or certain to happen. A father hopes that his daughter arrives at home safely after a visit, but hope doesn't bring clear weather or produce a defensive driver.

The institution of hope is a worldwide establishment that is incapable of anything we discuss in this book. Still, "We give people hope," is what advocates customarily say. Granted, this establishment can manufacture hope in short notice; the stark reality is that it can't even keep up with the bandaging.

You must understand, I am not demeaning the humanitarian investment by the deliberate cooperation of individual kindness. I emphasize "individual" to underscore that while corporations contribute, I recognize that it happens because of "individual kindness," behind the corporate names. The world applauds individuals who cooperate to support others in need. The issue isn't with the people supporting this idea— but it's in the idea itself.

Our posterity will not judge us on intent but, rather, on the traditions and consequences we pass onto them.

A subtle question remains unexposed. How much of this bandaging is for *wounds* beyond physical care? Not only that hope cannot keep up with human circumstances, it's only treating relatively insignificant wounds. Maintain the good work definitely, but society must recognize it for what it really does for humankind.

Like a powerful opiate, hope soothes our anxieties over aspects of life that we don't control, and gives us temporary relief until we know of the outcomes. Until I know that I pass my examination, I can hope that I will. Until our daughter calls us when she gets home safely, we may hope that she does. For what else do we hope? What else may hope be for us?

Hope is a deteriorating condition of trust, yet many people have come to accept it as a measure of human power.

The bigger the catastrophe, the bigger the hope. The more damage there is, the more people hope. The worse the battlefield, the sweeter the victory. It's a sort of mental warfare where people battle against human and extra-human forces, betting on who will win in the end.

Over the course of thousands of years, people build a sense of power into the notion; a sense of triumph due to the conditions required for hope to exist. Hope, for many people, is a mark of strength and how persistent they really are. Many people believe that while they are victims of desperate circumstances, they can still muster a remarkable measure of hope.

Some of these conditions include depression, despair, disheartenment, and disappointment. Other conditions are misfortune, dislocation, and dysfunction. People derive a sense of achievement, as they seem poised to prevail with hope over life's cruelest maladies.

People proudly instate a certain time of the year "tis the season of hope." It's a time when many people take it upon themselves to make miracles, believers, and wishful thinkers out of others. It's as if they try to deliver people from the miseries, which some believe God consigns. The consignment belief comes from the idea that "It's all a part of God's plan," of course.

The season of hope is a time when the sick receive attention, the hungry get love, the desolate become wishful, and apathy meets the red kettle and the bell ringer. It's also a time of greater pains for people who are already in anguish. It's a time of amplified loneliness, misfortune, and isolation; maybe because these people cannot afford to mask their pain with profusion. For many more people, it's a time of fruitless reflection, a time for regrets— a time to dread another pending year.

It's a time for another New Year's resolution. "I *hope* to God it works this time," as another year and another birthday pass, leaving only the painful reminders on our faces.

It's a time when all that remains for many people to do is introspect and examine the things that have gone wrong, to feel further desolation, for the sincerest human efforts turn up empty again. After all, whatever we tried, we did it earnestly to succeed. Most of us even coupled our sincere efforts with tireless and sanctified *hope*. Somehow, though, cruelty still casts its verdict once more.

Most people haven't figured out how to conquer and eradicate the conditions of despair, disheartenment, and dysfunction, so they disguise these conditions with the parade of hope. We all hope that goodness prevails and peace continues, then we take comfort in such hope— until another war breaks out.

Hope is a temporary eclipse of the conscious reality, a momentary closed-eye to appease the human need for denial. It's difficult, indeed, to fathom the adversities and, more critically, why they seem to torment innocent individuals.

The parade of hope is captivating. Everything is larger than life, and designed to look better than paradise. The running lights stir excitement that continues round after round, presumably forever. The repetitious and robotic gestures, such as waving, marching, and smiling, suggest timelessness and forbearance. Not to mention the extravagant costumes, and the people of flawless beauty they adorn. More treasured perhaps is the rhythm, which seems perfectly harmonious and inexorable.

Eventually, though, the untouchable displays all end, then we must take solace that the parade will resume when the season of hope returns. In the mean time, hope must last through another year.

We need to return again next year for more of the same thing, much like other dependencies requiring appeasement. This recurrence serves as a perennial shot for the habituated big-brain. People can suffer all year long with their own pains, but everyone can share in the return of the familiar parade of hope.

Hope requires uninviting conditions to exist.

If we take away pain, sorrow, despair, dislocation, and misfortune— hope cannot survive. How is it that such a sanctified notion thrives solely on the inescapable pains of its custodians? Is it to keep humankind in perpetual cycles of addiction and appeasement? Who would advocate a notion like hope?

What is the message of hope? Have we seriously reflected on it?

Poetry and rhetoric aside, for many people, hope means an entire life from birth to maturity and old age with a sense that what we wish for will come true. Hope is also desire accompanied by expectation. When hope doesn't materialize, many people put another check mark on the board to demonstrate the human patience, to underline their forbearance, and to show that their turn for favors is inevitably near.

Because God does not mettle, as we discovered from *The Human Struggle*, we understand that hope is but a spiritual game of statistics fabricated by the human mind, to keep people wanting and waiting.

Hope is similar to a form of psychological conditioning, used by scientists to induce compliance from experimental animals. In our case, we impose it upon ourselves. Because I missed out for the last 12 years, but continue to be patient, I should be getting my hopes fulfilled soon.

To put it concisely— hope means we don't know!

Consider the majestic Mount Rushmore in South Dakota, U.S. The financiers in the project may have doubted, wondered, and hoped that the colossal monument would bear the presidents' faces. The architect, however, knew that the enormous monument would bear the faces of the presidents. Accomplishments are not founded on hope.

An artist knows that his or her sculpture will be a bird, a man, or an abstract expression, even though bystanders and observers may suspect or hope for something else.

Hope pacifies people's anxiety due to human handicaps. On the other hand, knowledge removes the anxiety and offers alternatives to waiting for life's mercy.

We must learn to know, otherwise remain not knowing, but we must not substitute ignorance with something we valiantly call hope. Especially, as we have seen, when hope feeds on human anguish, for there is surely no victory in hope during times of gladness.

When people are in plenty, some do hope, too. "We can hope that good things continue. We can hope that good gets better," a writer tells me. Those are weak rationalizations, and mostly selfish when compared to the hope on anguish. It is selfish because, in plenty, people only hope that their accumulated materials never go away.

Instead of hoping that "good gets better," we should practice to become more sensitive, sincere, and communicative to God and one another. Instead of hoping that good gets better, humankind should better themselves. We must lessen our dependency on the improvements of human conditions. Instead, we should condition humans to improve.

Hope is passive and does not require accountability. Whether I did my homework, I can hope. I might have been dutiful or wasteful, I can hope. When things don't happen, I can increase the human power and hope more than before.

Hope does not require that we take any ownership and, in fact, offers a number of convenient absolutions. For example, "You're only human," or you have done all you can. "It's in God's hands now." Have some hope.

Invariably, hope has to be cyclical since it doesn't deliver. Numerous volunteers and countless hours of work go into the generation of hope, and millions of dollars pour into perpetuating the comfort that hope is everywhere. As long as we make a masquerade out of extravagance and perfection, even though only for a moment, it appears we have the real thing.

Who can resist the endless musical lights chasing tirelessly in perpetual merriment, and the rhythm of the marching bands in uniforms. Everything is in great rapport and agreement. The beat of drums, the synchronized progression, and the precision choreography all together make us yearn for the timeless excellence. It's as if the orderly succession were the wanting discipline in our lives.

What a catharsis it is!

People find comfort in the parade of hope because, unlike our own efforts, it appears that discipline can be harvested.

Other than being a passive habitual addiction, hope can fail and often does. Because it offers a consolation of its return, people overlook the fact that hope really is incapable of resolving any human plight.

Unlike working toward a goal and knowing the outcome, hope suspends us in an artificial contentment. Unlike understanding life's circumstances and optimizing our impact on our surroundings, hope suggests that someone else or another force will bring us the results.

We must conclude that hope is convenient, hope can be loud, hope can be displayed, and hope can be intensified. Hope involves millions of people and absorbs countless millions of dollars. All the financial and human costs add up to quite a premium, to merely afford people a temporary pass over life's maladies. When the moment is gone, or the season passes over, hope also dwindles away.

Hope cannot deliver us, while its pretense soothes us into believing that our sincerity and ignorance will move someone into shouldering it all for us. *The Human Struggle* shows that this sort of entrustment is not productive.

The most alarming thing about hope remains. It feeds solely on human wretchedness.

"Hope gives us strength!" you may protest.

Wait a minute. I thought people say that God gives you strength. Before we can progress and advance as a human race, we again need to resolve the conflicting beliefs within.

From whom do we draw our strength?

We must be consistent to prevail. If we say that God gives us strength and look for it in hope, what is our message? Doesn't God give people enough strength?

Suppose we elect to allow that hope gives people strength. Then for what is the next question.

Why do humans require so much strength?

Why do we need such an immense amount of strength, still, after thousands of years of hope?

Are we trying to move "a rock so big that *They* can't carry it"? Perhaps we've we been trying to move something God intended to stay put.

"We need strength to endure," I suspect many people may concede. We institutionalize our relationship with God, we raise the complexity of life, and confuse the promise of eternity, then use hope as a measure of endurance?

Why is enduring such a virtue anyhow?

The minute we endure, we need to ask ourselves "why?"

Rather than endure, we must understand. Instead of pacifying our anxiety, we need to know that goodness will dominate evil. Beyond asking our *Parents* to protect us, let us really believe that *They* do.

Some people may insist that "hope is a powerful emotion." I will remind you that fear, too, is a powerful emotion.

Let's consider eliminating the perennial shot notion, and work for the cure. While the established institution of hope can falter, we can regain our confidence and escape the bubble in language, thoughts, and achievements. After all, humankind comes from the highest possible lineage and the most resilient gene pool.

In our humbleness and humility at birth, we were endowed with the ultimate tools from Almighty God. We promised to be good stewards and execute fully our inborn capacities.

What are we waiting for?

The "parade" is only a symbolic depiction of the human bias for an underdeveloped notion of hope. While it is one way that we engage in self-fraud, there are numerous other methods and disguises people devise to appease their need for comfort in the absence of knowledge.

People pledge allegiance to God, submit to God, and ask God to care for them and protect them. Many people conceit that this is faith and entrusting, if you recall. Then, when people fall ill, they *hope* that they will get better. When people face a formidable opponent, they *hope* precariously for good luck. When people are fortunate, they *hope* it continues. When we pray to the omni-present and all-loving God, we *hope They* hear our prayers.

If we go as far as relinquishing everything for God, why is it that the best we can do is hope? Is entrustment merely a gesture of pretension after all?

When it comes to our personal lives, hope means we have not tended to the responsibilities to figure out our *selves*. Perhaps we have not completed the self-imaging task outlined in *The Essence*.

Hope— is that an act of wishing for something we have not, or wanting to connect to someone we do not know?

We can hope that it rains, while not knowing if it will. We can hope for the jackpot, because we are gambling. We can hope we make it, for we might weaken again.

Before God, consequently, hope echoes, "We don't know Thee still."

Let us abolish the "season of hope," and spring forth a new tradition of caring and forgiveness. Let's make this new tradition a life-long event. Demolish the institution of charity and build a new foundation for the research and examination of human suffering. Call it the foundation for human inquiry, where we can study the ailments and remedies for humanity.

Keep bringing coins to the red kettle and supporting local charities. More constructively, drop in to visit a friend on your way home. Comfort a brother and spend time building up one another, instead of pumping up hope. Make it a time for sharing a personal victory or an internal pain. Make it a time for belonging, and a time for aspirations. Make it a time that lasts all year long.

While the tangible objects of the material world might have veered us from the true light, we can correct the misdirection, remove our indirection, and realign with the beckoning Truth. Oh yes, it will take some time, effort, and planning. Unlike bandaging, though, we can nurse the real human pains.

We can abolish this establishment; we can eradicate life's maladies by mastering forward thinking and not just reactive philosophy. We will accomplish this with the power to decide vested in us at birth, and the essence we found through self-imaging.

We must believe that the power to decide is ours, if we're to spring into certain action.

God created us as free-thinking beings without condition, and independent decision makers in our own lives without exception. If the decision for our ultimate salvation is ours alone, invariably, all other choices are also ours. They must necessarily be so, because all choices are lesser than the choice of salvation.

Notwithstanding the reasoning, you might not depart from your insistence that your life is no more than a manifestation of destiny. Thus, regardless of what you may do, think, or decide, you contend to carry on a life in accordance with a written future. However you twist and turn, it works out in the end.

Destiny is obviously a theory I discourage, but perhaps due to its under-working that I, too, must allow you this latitude. In your destiny, I'm simply another scene in your explicit script. If you live as a "perfect" steward, this would be the place to stop my argument for fear of imperial contempt. You see, I err. Supposedly, you do not.

In either case, it does seem that you have the last word.

The first step toward resolving the predicament that hope has brought to humanity is to realize the power vested in us, and our ability to resolve the human predicament. We must then decide to trust rather than doubt, to know rather than hope.

From *The Image,* we're now able to envision the esoteric *Parents*. With the new perception, we now know the inner workings of Life. Because we have neither assembled the images of God nor, consequently, understood Life's secrets, we must consciously balance the need for proof and the obligation to heed the Truth.

The scientific *selves* in us demand tangible facts and digestible logic, while the spiritual selves count on us to simply hear the call beyond the bubble.

We must begin by putting God on our side. Being able to envision *Them*, we know that *They* aren't the ones who pulled the trigger at Columbine High School, sending friends and families to a week of funerals. We know that *They* didn't call for that unthinkable bomb truck in Oklahoma City on April 19, 1995.

Although we have not completely assembled, as prescribed by *The Image*, we have the required apparatus now to know.

We know the one God by projecting the humanity that we hold in our collective essences. We have seen the good in us, be as it may in partial assembly. We have seen the internal power and the iron will extruded from within, albeit in misdirection. Only that in our diffident past, we figured it all came from hope and prayers.

Knowing now that God is actually the One who entrusts in us, we promptly re-engage and honor the power bestowed in our humility at birth.

We must pledge to know so we can trust, and spare no expense toward that end. We shall learn where we lack knowledge; we shall seek that which we have not found, so that we can know, so that we can trust.

Let's abolish the "season of hope," and spring forth a new tradition of knowing. We know there is one God. We know we have the best tools. We know we're of the best gene pool. We know we have *Their* salvation.

We know— we have the final say.

With confidence, we know Life is permanent. We also know that the great human struggles we bear are consequences of an ignorant past. In knowing ourselves (by self-imaging), our God, our strengths, and our responsibilities, we know the prevalent good must triumph.

To know is to recognize what we don't know. We won't blunder at this, finally, because this step is error-free.

Beyond the first step, I *know* you will find the way, the means, and the *know*-how on your own. That way, you can be a witness yourself and bear live testaments to the glory of God, rather than reading about it from me, or reciting past testimonies.

What I am trying to convey here is that the practical answer to know lies in the recognition of hope. The key to victory lies in knowing the opponent. In understanding that hope is an addictive opiate, we know how to let it go. In realizing the conditions hope requires to exist, we know how to free ourselves from the shackling disillusion.

Once we discard hope, we know, and trust— rather than hope and doubt.

Keep in mind this one thought as we face, at times, insurmountable climbs. The problems we encounter are in themselves "human." We have the faculties to deal with them. We must develop and apply these faculties, lest our complacency distorts the relative magnitude of our hardships. When we stand still or digress, our troubles can appear to outpace our capacities to accept, understand, and manage.

If an extra-human problem were before us, we cannot know of it. When an event is beyond our perceptive capability, we cannot be cognizant of it. Give a five-year-old your income tax, and you'll see what I mean.

Can we perceive God-problems?

Be careful.

When *knowing* works for you, the world is a much more concrete place and Life can be comfortable, even if God doesn't bend the rules in our favor. Because we are in the know, we can trust and keep trust from deteriorating into hope. It's no longer a measure of performance as before. Our sense of achievement is redirected from the temporary suspense to the permanent journey.

We no longer fear the verdict of cruelty, for we do not wait for life's mercy anymore.

We know.

Knowing is self-sustained and does not require perennial booster shots for appeasement. Knowing swells and fills the void of "a sense that what we wish for will come true."

Knowing feeds on itself. It feeds on Life. It gives to Life, in contrast to the conditions that hope needs to survive.

Knowing is power and strength within itself, without a need for side insurance policies. Knowing is living or active, and communicable or contagious.

Knowing makes us active participants of Life— not just wishful spectators of hope.

So, what are we suppose to do with the annual parade down First Avenue? Keep it if you would like, but it is no longer the parade of hope for you.

Expecting something for nothing is
the most popular form of hope.
— Arnold Glasow

The Resolution

THE RESOLUTION

"To know is to recognize what we don't know. We won't blunder at this, finally, because this step is er-ror-free. "

— The Hope

The motivation of this book is to "offer practical answers to the apparent escalating evil around the world." As stated in *The Motivation*, my objective is to show that we can change the brittle world we live in, by altering its founding elements— or people.

We cannot endeavor to rid off societal ills merely by pushing social programs. People have seen that political stability cannot be maintained with policies alone. Neither science nor theology can ensure the survival of the human race in an increasingly complex world.

The meta-human *selves* must achieve harmony within each person, as individuals must arrive in concert on earth, if we're to reverse the destructive trend.

We begin this reversal by challenging the boundaries of peoples' minds, the extent of their experience and the possibilities they still need to perceive.

To achieve new understanding, we must be willing to read messages without imposing our successes and failures onto them. To arrive at new solutions, we must open ourselves to possibilities, to which our finite experience may not relate.

The Beginning revisits a traditional perception, and points out that as we are consisted of many *selves*, God is the ultimate multi-faceted Almighty. We must envision God as such, and uphold our vision consistently in thought and language.

While the language bubble doesn't have pronouns or words to adequately articulate God, it should not minimize *Them*— in speech, writing, or consciousness.

The Flat Mind reminds us that people might adamantly hold the earth to be flat, while it is very round. We might parade evidently where we stand, only to resort to saying "we're only human," when we fall. What people pledge to uphold so religiously for the moment can face the same test of consistency someday near.

We must allow the possibly that we have feared the wrong gods for thousands of years. We must accept that, maybe, what we have been so sure about, is not entirely about God.

The Origin insists that Life is a deliberate arrangement, in which we have a place, a role, and responsibilities.

Instead of instilling in generations the belief that this "place" isn't meant to last forever, people can permeate the fact that no living place remains unchanged. Rather than living for heaven and becoming tentative opportunists on earth, we can perpetuate the new idea that Life is eternal— that "it's the journey that matters in the end."

Not only must we live permanently, we must live loyally to one life. *The Monkey* rediscovers that we are the same children to our parents, as we are to God. To eliminate the disconnection between the double lives, we must live consistently.

From *The Monkey*, we also realize that institutions and regulations don't fashion intimate relationships, only communion does. We must live with understanding, trust, and love—not eulogies, and testimonies of writers or prophets.

Understand, distinctly, that people do not author God, in spite of how well they may write, translate, and interpret.

We don't need to regimen and complicate our lives with God, one another, and the "meta-selves" within. People don't need to use religions as certificates to spiritual superiority. Humans shouldn't use brain size to measure their thinking prowess. There is no need to introduce extraneous variables into our lives.

Instead, we must remove doubts from our lives, and instill knowledge as discussed in *The Inferiority*.

We must understand from *The Prophets* that Life deserves its own "itinerary," whether there is a prescribed ending. We should take on the permanent journey, and not live for the end. This, as we've learned, is because we can't define the extra-corporal end.

Believe that heaven is inevitable, but it is not the end.

We can now understand that choosing a physical or concrete end to strive for is good planning. *The Heaven* explains that because we cannot define the ethereal, it is an ambiguous end for which to "justify the means."

While we cannot determine heaven for sure until we get there, we should be very certain of what we expect from its new inhabitants.

As we look to heaven, we see many impressions of our own religious upbringing, and the circumstances that compound the kingdom we're trying to understand. Needlessly, dogma seems to have turned the vice on us.

We agree that perception governs most aspects of people's lives, from the basic thread of understanding to the building blocks of tradition, and consequently our comprehension of God. *The Dogma* leaves no doubt that religious doctrines have the largest monopoly on the human perception thus far. To re-establish independent thinking and free people's perception, and to enhance our reception of God, we must take charge and break away from dogma's grip.

We should use teachings and traditional language as training wheels. One day, we will need to graduate from the simple balancing act and adopt directional control, to take advantage of the maneuverability that comes with free ride. Only by removing the once helpful system can we achieve the freedom to lean, turn, swerve, and not merely wobble precariously— in spirituality.

We can understand that training wheels were necessary, but certainly cannot see how we could ever ride with them now. They even look dangerous to us. What would happen if one of them were to drop into a pothole, or go up on a curb? What if I need to lean and avoid an obstruction quickly, or ride on a narrow trail?

What if I am too big for them?

The freedom without wheels has its many scars, but we all ride much larger bicycles today, and fully control where we go.

What changed us from hanging on to those wheels one day to looking at them as crutches now?

Like the nervous balancing act, we have to let go of our fear to stand up against forces that make us fall. Like the vertical ride we later pulled off, there's no way we can lift ourselves up to God until we trust, no matter how much we remain in practice. Many Christians, for example, regularly sing vibrantly: "We lift them to the Lord," but clearly demonstrate that they trust the ground more firmly.

Understandably, we embraced the training wheels then but, at an appropriate time, we took away their chance to become a liability. They could no longer tip us over at the curb, drop us into the potholes, and ultimately hold us back.

Once you are on the right vehicle and in complete control, the world becomes an entirely different place. New destinations will avail themselves, including those you may have concluded unreachable before.

To see what I mean, pedal your bicycle to a familiar shop or workplace where you have only reached by car in the past. A bit treacherous, you may discover. To better illustrate the point, ride a donkey to a destination where you have only arrived by plane.

Aside from self-emancipation, we must have the courage to insist that credible ideas must pass the consistency test. When we remove contradictions, Life becomes a more permanent dimension in our minds. Permanency returns as the new governor and a lasting fabric of life.

Let us also stop the maiming of people on the human side of the battlefield, as was appealed in *The Paper Plate*.

Let's start a new social etiquette in which it's deplorable to consider Life as temporary.

Everyone can account for their own permanent lives without doubts by knowing. Accountability, driven by the permanent mindset, leads to confidence and ownership in Life.

Free perception backed with knowledge changes how we experience the permanent journey.

The world's sufferings cease to crumple us in pain, when we know the key to the human struggle. The two original elements of this key promise to liberate people from disparaging circumstances of corporal life. "Don't include God in our struggles," is one element outlined in *The Human Struggle*.

"Knowing now that God is actually the One who entrusts in us," is the other element of this key.

Entrustment now means God's confidence in humankind, rather than people's exploitative enlistment of *Them*.

The Image de-mystifies God and affirms that we are *Their* fragments. Until now, many people have merely been estimating who God is, based on human experience with requests and expectations.

When I ask God to help me win the lottery, I end up losing another dollar. I might think that God's not into gambling. When I pray for a loved one to never die, and find myself weeping over the irreversible loss, I might think that maybe God doesn't like favoritism. This estimation goes on, as we have been approximating God for thousands of years.[1]

Unlike people's continuous reconstruction of God, *The Image* reveals that we only need to reconstruct the images of ourselves. This can be done by self-imaging, and eliminates the need to estimate our esoteric *Parents*.

When we identify the essences beginning with our conception, along with those we come to embrace, we can build the fundamental basis of who we each are. From *The Essence*, we can achieve accord with the *selves* within, and love the individual our essences embody.

---

[1] Taken from *The Human Struggle.*

The more intimate we are with our essences, the more we can tend to them and recognize them individually. We can know which forces are at work, which forces are dormant, and which forces are imagined.

This respectful love for the self, from understanding and knowing, does not stop at the personal boundaries, as it also permeates to others. We now can translate the love for the selves within to a love for others. Only when I have learned to sanction my essences and love me, can I possibly fulfill the same for another.

Eventually, we may come closer to truly loving God.

People show that as we have, we tend to give— and as we are, we tend to inspire.

Now is the time for me to offer you the First Commandment Revisited:

Know your essence— for it's in your *Parents'* essence that you are.

This is the new human imperative!

Until we assume the posture of our essence, we do not know who we are. We cannot know who God is.

If you do not figure out your essence, you're bringing nothing to God.

Some people might have a point in contending that the First Commandment Revisited encourages already rampant selfish abuses. Let me offer a reason for assurance:

I understand we are all resistant to change or, more precisely, the methods of change. The answer to the question of abuse is that people are envious only for what they are not, and greedy for what they don't have. Concern not about others, for if they abuse, it's not this imperative that they fulfill.

Irrefutably, "Know your essence— for it's in your *Parents*' essence that you are," is fundamentally correct and spiritually upright, because we cannot abuse it. For every person who is enriched in the image of God, by finding his or her essence, God rejoices and reclaims another child.

Let us all exploit the First Commandment Revisited!

Remember, people who have, tend to give. People who are, tend to inspire.

Could you give joy if you don't have joy? Could you encourage others in diffidence?

The First Commandment Revisited is virtuous, self-maintaining, and self-policing. In it is the essence of humanity. In our assembly, therefore, is God.

To fail this directive is to come short of knowing the one person we must know to achieve the knowledge threshold to know God.

We must achieve the First Commandment Revisited, as we're also expected to, "Love our neighbors as ourselves."

Recall from *The Hope*: Knowing is self-sustained and does not require perennial booster shots for appeasement. Knowing swells and fills the void of "a sense that what we wish for will come true."

Even with the knowledge, where do we begin?

Deterioration doesn't happen overnight, neither does restoration. Corrosion eroded everything in succession over thousands of years as illustrated in this book. We should expect to reinvest a serious amount of time, if we intend to rebuild thoughtfully.

The beauty of *The Resolution* is that the reconstructions can happen simultaneously. I can work on *The Flat Mind,* while you work on *The Monkey.* We can get our families involved in *The Prophets* and *The Heaven,* and more.

All this we do to fulfill, if nothing else, this one directive:

"Know your essence— for it's in your *Parents'* essence that you are."

Some day soon, we can all sing spontaneous songs, not just reproduced hymns. Befriend God, rather than behold *Them.* Commune with God, and not merely of *Them.*

Only in our glorious becoming, will God be satisfactorily glorified.

Because most people are meticulous, I must applaud their skepticism when enticed with a good offer or an appealing plan. I suspect that some people might question, "What do we do about the devil, who is ready to ruin any accomplishment humankind might endeavor?"

No plan is complete without preparing for interference, disruption, and contingency. We will face significant obstacles, be they terrain, one another, or the devil.

Can we out-maneuver darkness?

More than maneuver, we can eliminate the devil, as you'll see.

Let's put our conviction and training to the test, and fulfill *The Resolution.* After all, we have the means, the power, and the big brain— if we could just see the way.

You must be the change you wish to see in the world.
— Mahatma Gandhi

The Devil

THE DEVIL

<blockquote>
"Do humans really have a mechanism to isolate the devil's work— as opposed to the work of an ailing brother or sister? We are pompous fools if we think that we have been thwarting the forces of Satan.

Do you, your religion, and its teachers soberly believe you can withstand a physical, much less spiritual, blow from Satan?"

— The Dogma
</blockquote>

To be consistent I will again break traditional norms by restraining from launching a difficult campaign full of definitions. People are more or less experts about the devil, specifically the evil underwriting we regularly witness. I'll also leave the meaning of "evil" up to you.

It's important to note that many schools of thought believe evil is a necessary part of good. They contend that there must be black before people can discern white, dark to see light, and bad so we may arrive at good.

We must insist that God's glorious heaven is not a negative polarity of hell. We must maintain that some people are not hell-ridden merely so that other people can be heaven-bound. Recall from *The Dogma,* "God does not share the other side of the coin with the devil."

Let's believe that goodness doesn't have to be a bad contrast, if you will.

Otherwise, if there's no bad, what good is it? It's like the ticker marks on the side of a boat, where the higher the water mark, the deeper the boat is in the water. To be most "good"— must we sink?

While we might not agree on words and definitions, we can find and share vivid images of the devil's work. These accounts and images have a disturbing common denominator; they cause levels of anguish to humankind.

The purpose of the devil's toiling doesn't play an important role in this book, because the need to live in the light still challenges us, even if he mettles without purpose. People tend to fixate on the intent, while his slight of hand continues to humiliate us throughout the millennia.

We must caution that the devil has unimaginable powers coupled with a cruel willingness to discharge torture.

People from all parts of the world have stories of evil inclemency to tell throughout human history. While this kind of storytelling can serve as a catharsis to our incapacity and dreadful guilt, I use it, in this book, to illustrate his machinery of fear and despicable cowardice.

Storytelling hasn't helped very much, unfortunately, even though people tell more stories now, with tradition, literature, and the media. There's so much news in mailboxes, so many television shows through cables, and radio broadcasts over airwaves; the stories are only becoming more horrific and more frequent.

While we might not be the source of the anguish, we often feel a tremendous responsibility and frustration, and are compelled to help however we can. For example, people expressly give to subsidize crime-fighting efforts in communities. Some of us give quietly to support drives to end hunger. Others give to heal distant wounds in third world countries. There are those who can give only through prayers, for they too have suffering and afflictions.

Some people can barely give the promise of tomorrow, but many give to say we're united, that we will not stand watch— that hand in hand "we are the world. "

Yet the sick are still dying, the famished are still hungry, and the persecuted are still silent, while people invest increasingly more resources into resisting world disorders. One look around and we see the perils of life lurking in readiness to isolate, frustrate, disappoint, and dishearten us.

Relief efforts are now more organized and effective than ever before, but we are not stopping hunger or fending off diseases. Keep in mind, too, that the United States is not the only charitable source, if we are to understand the humanitarian investment.

Earlier, people charged that it's all a part of God's plans for the transgressions against children, between brothers and sisters, and all other human anguish escapable only in hindsight. God will ultimately claim responsibility when the dust settles, many people believed.

Now it seems that we are more content seeing the devil taking the blame. Some people are still uncomfortable about charging God then accusing the devil, so they opt for mediation to add that the devil, too, must be part of God's plan.

Most of us get particularly frustrated when the devil is utterly void of sportsmanship. Why doesn't he have the audacity to level his evil against someone his own size, or someone who has comparable powers? Why is he such a coward, attacking children, weak, and innocent people?

Granted there are those among us who aren't so innocent, but that, again, is because the devil contaminated them. Nonetheless, we vow to feed our own hunger, and nurse our own wounds, while unknowingly fuel his machinery of fear.

In anguish, people can become agitated and easily frustrated over the increasing perils we face in life, which bring us apprehension and fright.

People grow up fearing the devil and his destruction. Most people are told that he is powerful, inhumane, and murderous, and that he must be avoided at all times. He will fool you, sucker you, mock you, and ruin you. Tradition and doctrine tell us, "You are no match for him." Beware!

It boils down to this. His machinery of fear requires human anxiety and agitation to run. He fails if he can no longer inflict apprehension and fright.

Religious doctrines leave us without the critical apparatus to discern, initially, between God's plans and humans' adaptations; and, now, between human mistakes and evil schemes. Thus, we too have doubts about the devil's work, for we do not *know* for sure. Is it the devil's wickedness, God's plan, or just humans' practices?

You may be surprised to know that there's no need to identify whether it's the devil's work, for we deceptively possess yet a more lethal weapon.

Let me explain.

We give the devil an irresponsible amount of attention and praise, albeit negative. Human tragedies continue around the world for various reasons but, for the most part, we really don't know why. Charged with emotion and scant information, many people quickly assign the misfortunes to the evil underworld.

The devil gets the credit for the terrors indiscriminately and almost immediately.

When this terrorist strikes, we attribute responsibility, or praise, before he even has a chance to claim it. Political terrorists must use a phone, identify themselves, and claim responsibility, but not the devil. When it appears that he terrorizes, we simply hand him the signed certificate of success, and dutifully broadcast his effectiveness worldwide.

For the vast majority of us, this attribution is really a natural reflex. For example, it takes a number of jurors to make a modern justice system work, while people would burn the devil at the stake without deliberation. How have we been deciding who has committed a crime?

The devil doesn't necessarily come out in his flame suit to terrorize us. Many people believe that he hires or possesses people like you and me to carry out his evil plans for him. At least, that's what most people have believed and taught for a few thousand years.

How do people decide who to burn? How do people maintain their conviction rate time and time again in a spiritual high court?

There is a true justice system where we can condemn the devil precisely, convincingly, and honorably. The awesome power in this system is that we can do it without error!

Here's how it works: Suppose the devil causes a person to suffer, we promptly claim responsibility for the misdeed. I know this sounds awkward, considering the way we have been reacting instead, but let's get together on this. Unlike demented human terrorists, the devil cannot get on national television to fight us for credit.

I suspect some people are thinking that he gets on national television by hiring strayed human beings in his place.

Fine, but disregarding what, how, or if he could claim, we insist that the responsibility for the aggression is ours. Yes sure, he used my knuckles to punch my brother in the nose, but I am not letting the devil take credit this time, or ever again.

"Sorry brother, I'm a loser for bringing you pain and embarrassment." Tell your brother or sister how you will restrain yourself against such cruel injuries, how you will not be used next time.

Obviously, we might not succeed the first attempts, while we work diligently to undo millennia of practice in the failed justice system. Soon, we'll get proficient enough to condemn the devil precisely, convincingly, and honorably, without error.

Whether a human perpetrator operates independently or as the devil's instrument, there is no longer a need to discern who's who in the new justice system.

What if no one is there to take responsibility away from the devil when a person is victimized? If the victim is you, you know what to do. Get up and say, "I hurt myself." Yes, this maybe uncomfortable, but nobody's there, supposedly, to ridicule you.

We deprive the devil's chances to claim responsibility.

Because we're all in this campaign together, another person would also know what to do, when he or she is a victim when no one else is around. As with *The Image* and previous chapters, we all need to participate because we have a shared obligation.

It's time we get rid of this terrorist with no further negotiations.

I maintain that in prolonged human sanctions such as this one, the devil would wither and perish, because that which sustains him is gallantly withheld. There is no need for spiritual warfare or divine intervention, as *The Human Struggle* concluded not to exploit prayers and God's services anymore.

There's no need— finally— for blame.

To clarify, that is blaming God for not meeting our expectations, and blaming Mister D for possibly human flaws.

Rob his fire!

Let us take away his thunder.

Every man and woman solemnly monitors and promptly claims every one of his or her evils, big and small. Before the devil knows he has accomplished something, we take it away. Before he gets to the microphone, we turn off the tape. Every father for his children and every mother for hers, make a vow to their heirs to honorably and unwaveringly assume all evils that are understandable, as well as those we cannot comprehend.

We must agree that our children should not be condemned to live with another failed coup.

Don't start thinking about grisly acts of human transgression yet. While I share your enthusiasm and urgency, let us start with smaller violations that don't make the news. These are crimes against the family and individuals, infesting in homes and in backyards.

If we succeed at this sanction, the devil will not be increasing the difficulty level of his games, if you will.

Suppose you had a bad day at work starting with a frustrating meeting. When you are finally on your way home, you suddenly remember that you need to stop at the market. Because your day was not spectacular, other mishaps could creep up too, you know. "Hey, there's a parking space close to the door. I'll quickly park in there, and hurry on to beat the rush."

Minutes later, you proceed toward the cashier. "Oh my goodness, look at the lines," you think as you shuffle from one counter to another in search of quick service. There's an unsuspecting person who seems to be in no hurry over there, you notice. You don't know the person but casually pull up from the side, paste your eyes intently on a tabloid, and cut in conveniently where the newsstand incidentally narrows the path.

"How slow can people be," you murmur. "No one can expect me to waste my time lining up behind them," you might protest in your head. However, you do feel some guilt so you quiet yourself with, "everybody else does it, too." "I'm inherently a good person though. I've been banking all my favors. The devil must have the best of me tonight. He always knows when I'm tired. He always pushes me at the right time."

Boom.... Bang.... Smack! You have just slapped another "certificate of success" into Mister D's hand. He walks off with the blue ribbon again. Congratulations, shopper! You can now move to the next level of difficulty in his games. Ding... ding.

No. That is not your turn at the register. The dings come from the adjacent lane, and a stranger is looking at you. You know what, she said, "I know you saw me signaling for that parking space out there." Shaking her head, she continues, "But I'm not going to say the devil drove you into it. I expect you to claim responsibility." she says as she turns and walks away.

Acknowledge when we mess up, so we can recognize it when the devil comes again.

Apologize to the person you injured or, at least, regret the transgression. You must also look at what you have done as the executor of someone's will. Yours, or the devil's? Look at it again. How does it defeat another person? How does it disrespect another human being? How you must see it coming next time around.

We all must rise and accept our "evils"— lest the devil feasts on them, and laugh at our devices.

That's right. We pick up the small stuff, so it cannot pile up into mountains, which we cannot move or cover up. We cannot erect enough walls. We cannot wire enough fences. We cannot move far enough from each other. We mustn't forget that we eventually need to assemble, in order to see God.

Remember, we need to respect the importance of smaller goals, if we endeavor to accomplish mission impossible. This also applies to the devil. If he cannot get people to overtake one another's parking space, or cut in front of one another waiting in line, he will have a hard time convincing people to strike against anyone.

If the devil cannot get you to curse at your spouse or children, he doesn't have the words for domestic abuse. If he cannot get you to slander a neighbor, he doesn't have the weapon to assault a human being.

This also is how we implode darker plumes of evils such as child pornography and prostitution, in the long run. For every child that suffers, we withhold a reward. For every woman who's violated, we deny a blue ribbon. For every single offense against humanity, we pull one breathing tube. For a slayed brother or sister— we remove his life support.

What an arsenal we have!

What kind of weapon have you been searching for? Do you realize how we have forsaken our sovereignty? We have been hiding in fear, in shame, and in cubbyholes of our own jurisdiction.

What human transgressions can't people claim? To what sovereignty can the devil assume that we must yield? What terrible human condition are we afraid to withhold from him?

The devil might as well know that we're all cooperating to reclaim our responsibilities as workers and custodians of Life, and to regain the dominion handed to us since the beginning.

Deceptively or otherwise, Mister D, we're now armed!

We might each be a sheep before God, the Shepherd in whom we shall not want. We will continue to perish before the devil as lambs. Do people really believe that he can't tell when humans are petrified in doubt and disconnection? We don't think that we can shake the devil with lip service, do we?

Forget about beware. Do better— *en garde*!

What kind of wolf do people suppose we, the sheep, are dealing with?

Defend our right to spiritual patriotism. Defend our children's right to childhood innocence. Defend Life's caravan, and reinforce our permanent journey. By so doing, we shall jealously secure the arrival of the human race.

Let's take away his fire.

Here's an incredible story and a stupendous catharsis to share and, more importantly, an extraordinary insight into the human struggle. We will use it as our traveling companion, as we aim to complete the permanent journey. The following is interpreted from the *King James Bible*, Isaiah 14:12-19 and Ezekiel 28:12-18. The original text is enclosed in the Appendix.

> Once upon a time... far, far back into an immeasurable past, there were no people, and there was no relationship. There was simply no love. For as many tribulations as there seems now, the void of that past must have seemed much more desolate. So, as many believe, God was driven to create

angels to occupy *Their* kingdom, and to fill the heavens with joyful songs from nations of angelic hosts.

In particular, there was one angelic being who garnered the pinnacle of combined wisdom and immaculate beauty, which heaven and earth had never seen. He was the perfect culmination made possible only by the favor of God. It is written that he was appointed to God's celestial garden where God tills the heavenly soil, sows *Their* thoughts and reflections— and cultivates *Their* innermost essences.

The angel was ornamented with precious fortunes, for his body was inlaid with priceless gems, which brought together the most remarkable assembly of tangible richness. They expounded testimonies about how God adored him and sealed his beauty with that of *Their* own.

Each of his stones was of natural and exquisite formation. How colorless were they, as he was unassuming; translucent, as he was unclouded; yet reflected great lights, as he resonated in arrays of colors from pale-blue to deep-blue, and pale-green to sea-green, and bright-green, and red, and more.

He was irrefutable, as his stones were second in hardness only to diamonds, which also adorned him. The sapphire's blue was so deep, as he was profound, all beneath the white or sincerity, yellow or friendship, and purple or valor, array of colors.

His diamonds were unflawed, as he was perfect; beryl was rare, as he too was one of a kind;

and amethyst prevented drunkenness— as we knew him to be sober and temperate among angelic hosts. In their varieties, the precious stones explicated his invariable virtues and glaring distinction.

Stones from stones as onyx were of agates, while jaspers were of quartz, and topaz were of sapphires. Colors from colors as each were radiantly dispersed from their crystalline properties. They were all distinct, as he was multifaceted; yet, in assembly a homogeneous assortment.

Some stones were transparent and colorless yet inertly brilliant and full of colors, as he was uncomplicated but entirely wholesome. Others were translucent and impenetrable, for he also was private and custodial. All were otherwise seen set only in gold, on breastplates of high priests since then.

At least, that is how we'd have to recount him in revealing and retelling his blinding glory. He was not physically of stones, but only the most precious and brilliant of all ethereal combined could describe him.

To amplify his magnificence was his inborn faculties for symphonic production, as if he was accessorized with rhythmical drums and resounding pipes from when he was created.

God appointed him specifically for his allegiance to *Their* holy garden, and to its complete protection and defense. God placed him on *Their* high mountain, and he did march victoriously in fiery combats.

He was ever so perfect until, sudden, his fortunes and mounting material possessions filled him with discord.

No further glorification was necessary as he had fantasized about an ascension, through his own power and brilliance. Whereby heightening the status of his throne above the all-powerful spotlights of even the almighty God. Additionally, he would assume the chairman's place, as if to guide and to rule the congregation of nations [of angels]. Finally, he would ascend past all possibilities, above all skies, beyond which there could be no other—but he alone.

In a moment of fantasy, it's like he would be "the most high"; higher than God.

Before he could come to it, he was charged and sentenced to a life of homelessness at the edges of the dark dominion. Because of his partiality or inequity, God swiftly disconnected him, particularly, from the inner mysteries or esoteric knowledge of God. *They* discharged him from the high mountain on which he was once placed. "I will destroy you," said God, "in the same fiery battles in which you were earlier victorious."

He apparently corrupted his wisdom by his reasoning ability, and by succumbing to his glamorous brilliance and celebrity status. I will revoke the fierce power of flight from your wings (all six or nine of them) and expose your inequity before your peers, God scolded, so they too may experience and learn from your departure.

Adding insult to injury, he trampled over his holiness, violated his essence, and consequently the essence of God by the gravity of his betrayal.

In complete indignation God promised, "I will command fires to turn you into ashes of the ground, from which all onlookers shall heed."

"Oh… my faithful gardener, defender of my thoughts and reflections, keeper of my innermost essences— oh my anointed confidant," cried God.

Those that saw him, gazed at him with intolerance, prejudice, and judgment. Is this the one that caused the tremors and brought doubts into the nations, who upset the established rule of law; the one who brought disarrangement to the established discipline and the resultant destruction? Is this the one whose fall is so sudden and swift that all unwary bystanders die while sleeping under their own wings?

Far from the last nail in the coffin, he was forced out of his grave like an outcast among the dead, at sword-point by the ghostly garments of the slain. Not having even the refuge of his own grave, he was "trodden under feet" in perpetuity. Ultimately, one day, he too will be under abusive pressures, compressed into, ironically, stones similar to those that long ago graced his forever-lost beauty.

Behold, his glorious and brilliant essence, or heart, was spared because he was the pinnacle of the perfect culmination made possible only by the favor of God.

Everything else except his "heart" became the embodiment of a shattered dream. The fall of this angel brought the angelic orders their first and only loss ever known in heaven. From wings to wings devastated angels mourned, "Oh you son of the morning... stars of the dawn... how could you possibly fall from Eden, the garden of God? How is it possible that incredible flight has been taken from your mighty defender's wings, impairing and exposing nations!"

It was a humiliating and crippling loss with strategic ramifications all over the ether-realms.

An angelic supreme, second only to God— has fallen.

No more immaculate beauty, no more perfect culmination, no more glaring distinction, as the blinding glory stops.

This tragic event later triggered the fall of humankind. The fallen angel, Lucifer, or Satan, as he was called, vowed to take you, me, and our wretchedness into perpetuity.

Fragments of his broken wings continue to land on human frailties and our dependency on spiritual leadership. Many of us have good reasons to believe that he rose to power again to rule as the vengeance lord of the outcasts, misfits, and the meek. Recognizing our need for spiritual leadership, he feeds us "hope and appeasement."

He manages to have people believe that hope comes from faith in God, while it's probably he who casts doubt and distributes shame. It's likely he who brings disconnection, which he knows all too well, and unveils for us the sense of renewal in hope.

It's as if he deprives us of something that is ours, only to tease us with appeasement, and watch us turn willingly into hope-junkies.

His mission, it seems clear, is to reap havoc and force defections in the earthly nations, to expand his tyranny, and to eventually reclaim a garden of old. It must seem only fair to him that we do not make it back to our *Parents*, if he can never have such an opportunity himself.

Inevitably, it appears, humankind has the daunting task of reckoning with a very capable super-power in its midst.

As it is consistently written, God does not intervene in Satan's bloody rampage to "mount the congregation." Wherever Satan is mentioned in the Bible, we can also find clear evidence that God doesn't stop him from inflicting on us, for the most part. It's as if Satan also doesn't live in a pre-programmed life.

Over the course of time, it became increasingly more apparent that he wasn't going to relent, thus we might have to fold under his dark shadows. Some of these shadows, sadly, resemble those of our own, as humanity stands bewildered. It's sweet revenge for him, perhaps, because people lack the cohesion and strength of a unibody.

At least, so he thinks.

We, too, were endowed by our esoteric *Parents*, whence we were also "accessorized" with a direct connection with God. In humbleness, we re-discover our weapons. In humility, we understand our mission. With the vigor of righteousness, we're ready to act.

We do not recognize any prince— not even the prince of darkness. We do not hail any other's accomplishments, except those of our Almighty God. We do not hand out blue ribbons anymore, for we will need them to decorate each other.

As asserted earlier, "the need to live in the light still challenges us, even if he mettles without purpose," or whether the devil mettles at all. We must take full claim and immediate responsibility for anguishing events in human life. Our sanction of raw materials against the devil is not a meditated vindictive engagement, but we act, as we must, to ultimately hone our own virtues.

We realize that, otherwise, we're giving nothing to God.

Let's stand up, stewards of God. Recognize one Almighty God, who is the God of light and truth and triumph. Renounce recognition and notion of all other rulers, entities, or names of any other dominion. There is no need to renounce the devil, if people don't recognize him in the first place.

By virtues of disassociation— the devil will be disconnected for the last time.

We can remove Satan from "our dependency on spiritual leadership" by removing our occupation with the devil, and by nourishing our relationship with God. By claiming responsibilities and living up to our capacity, we put a stop to the human struggle. By picking up the slack or taking ownership, and by recognizing where we might trip again or learn from our mistakes, we can be ready participants every time threats lurk.

One day, there will be no more sustainable evil, for the one we charge with conspiring darkness will be no more.

Interestingly, that *one day* came long ago.

You see, while people struggle to re-enter the garden of God, they lose sight of the basic requirements for returning to heaven. Most people believe that faith and repentance are the qualifying ingredients to God's kingdom. If we knew enough about our *Parents*, faith would exceed its bounds and become knowledge, and repentance would become respect.

God's lieutenant has this level of esoteric "knowledge." No other was closer to God than Lucifer, "Star of the dawn."

By the time humankind was created and learned to cast judgment about him, Lucifer had long returned, because it's only a matter of time with all of God's creations.

Many people demonize Satan, and believe that they can muster enough faith to enter the kingdom of God. That's assuming, of course, that people can be sincerely penitent.

Because Lucifer had esoteric advantage, his faith would exceed its bounds and become knowledge. He doesn't need creeds and religions to inspire him. People need to search for faith. He simply puts himself back in the *know*. People need time to repent. He has time. Really, how long do we estimate it would take Lucifer in his "full wisdom and perfect beauty"[1] to accomplish the same thing, in spite of popular human beliefs?

Maybe more than you and I, Lucifer is also a child of the all-loving Almighty God.

While we only rank among peers, this is a good place for some humbleness, to accept the relative strength, capacity to trust, and will power between Lucifer and us. If humankind can repent, we must concede that Lucifer has done it.

Let's liberate ourselves from the pre-occupation with this phantom criminal, so that we can remove our shackles and stop the presumptuous finger-pointing.

---

[1] Ezekiel 28:12, *King James Bible*

Especially dangerous is when people point fingers at someone who isn't there. Obviously, we do no harm to him, but what a disgrace to humanity.

Someone has the faculty to repent, and God has the love to forgive.

Do we dare to doubt either of these powers?

Do we dare to decide that God only forgives us?

Until we let go of the original grudge, there may be no escaping the original sin.

Maybe it's too much to ask the human mind to realize that the devil was constructed, over the course of millennia, by the human need to shelter themselves from the judgmental eye of God. The devil is a human-made spiritual dump. If God ever asks, "What's that smell?" people can all turn and point at the refuse.

We must change our literature, modify our thoughts, and introduce new methods of managing our perpetrators, handling our weaknesses, and controlling our tendency to blame. The devil doesn't exist; the spiritual dumpsite is now closed. Educational institutions needs to direct their negative energy elsewhere, and stop blaming human conditions on the devil. The world must wake up and take responsibilities for human tragedies, and armies must carry blood on their own hands every time they kill yet another.

No trigger man— no fall guy.

When the devil is removed from humanity, we can reconstruct peace, for we now know better than to cast blames. When the devil is removed from humanity— then we can get on with Life's permanent journey.

We must stop the smears, slanders, and insults now, before the lieutenant of God decides that we are annoying. We never could have withstood an offensive blow from him. We never could withstand his torment. Beware, we can much less withstand a defensive coup from Lucifer.

If we could get away from our flat-mind, there is no higher ally than Lucifer. There is no one who can better relate to the human struggle, for he has been there, and back.

What if I am wrong?

Have you thought about it?

First, I am not writing to seek glory in my own righteousness. I am writing to call on you to reconsider how you want to prepare for your return to your *Parents*, and whether you can break away from the human spiritual trappings.

Still, you may insist, "What if I am wrong?"

I have a better question for you: What if you can't forgive?

Perhaps, we are the ones who choose not to amend.

What does it mean to us on this earth if people cannot forgive? Life will unfold one day at a time, as it always has, and human transgressions will continue to entertain the evening news. People will still have the devil to blame for the world's evil.

Inevitably, *The Human Struggle* thrives.

You know, while people can digress, I wouldn't bet on Lucifer doing the same. We have an opportunity now to rise above our past— and elevate humanity.

Notwithstanding, if the devil must live in your mind, you know what to do.

As I stated earlier, you take away his fire.

The penalty for embracing the fall-guy notion is an eternity in groundless blame, perpetual persecution, and self-denial. Additionally, we would have to count on God to return, because we will need to be carried again, like the "Footprints in the Sand."[1]

Be careful! The one to shoulder us might be the one people condemn.

The world will not see complete harmony until all of God's children have returned to *Them*. There will be no feast as long there is still suffering by anyone. I challenge the most studious scholars to disagree, to glorify an all-loving God, yet accept a feast in heaven amid even one anguishing cry from below, or from inside.

Unless we stand tall and look on, as the world turns so will the blind eye of human denial— and blame will be our perpetual absolution device.

Let it go.

Finally, think of a young child who is trying to stop stealing, a mid-life man losing to alcoholism, or a parent whose moments are near. Do you know anyone like that? Can you think of someone in a similar circumstance?

A touching peculiarity is that they would have perished much earlier in their battle, if no one had faith in them. People like you and me, from the glamorous to the destitute, have absolutely no reason to try, to achieve or, in some cases, to even

---

[1] The *Footprints in the Sand* is a poem by Mary Stevenson, which many people enjoy for its depiction of God carrying humankind over tribulations.

live— if no one trusts that we are able to overcome our predicament.

Have you ever decided that your climb isn't worth the effort if you must climb alone, or if everyone thought you would die trying? Maybe no one would wait for you at the top of your climb.

You may understand the power of trusting and knowing, if someone has ever doubted or discounted you. Your best friend *thinks* you will make it. Your mother *hopes* you will win. Worse yet, you may pray for luck, while your friend splits the bet on someone else.

Let's change all of that around. Your best friend *trusts* that you will make it to the top. Your mother *knows* you will win.

I understand that many people are highly disciplined. These people think that the more others disbelieve, the more determined and accomplished they become.

The fallen angel has returned, "determined and accomplished," before humans can catch on.

You see, Lucifer had just about the whole world disbelieving in him.

Though disconnected, Lucifer could repent, if not by his own strength, because someone believed in him— the mourning angels during Lucifer's terrible fall, the trying angels who filled his shoes, or the human race that followed. Somewhere in the vast ethereal or the unlikely earth, someone believed in him.

Tragic as it may be, perhaps no one has believed in Lucifer. How would you like to be the catalyst for the return of the biggest prodigal son in God's kingdom?

No! I am not talking about your personal glory.

I am talking about PEACE.

When you feel doubt, overwhelmed, and disconnected, just look up to the son of the morning, and follow his example of courage[1]. He did it without self-maiming, and he did it without blaming.

When our wretchedness seems unrelenting, perhaps we can invigorate ourselves; for we, like no others, have a superior and perfect ally who can relate to the power of repentance—and the indubitable mercy of God.

---

[1] "Lucifer" means light of the morning (Job 50:17), or son of the morning (Isaiah 14:12)

POINTS OF REFLECTION

There's no need—finally—for blame.

One day, there will be no more sustainable evil, for the one we charge with conspiring darkness will be no more.

Until we let go of the original grudge, there may be no escaping the original sin.

Tragic as it may be, perhaps no one has believed in Lucifer.

I am talking about PEACE.

— The Devil

When one rows, it is not the rowing
that moves the ship.
Rowing is only a magical ceremony
by means of which,
one compels a demon to move the ship.
— Friedrich Nietzsche

The Final Victory

THE FINAL VICTORY

"The world will not see complete harmony until all of God's children have returned to Them. *There will be no feast as long there is still suffering by anyone. I challenge the most studious scholars to disagree, to glorify an all-loving God, yet accept a feast in heaven amid even one anguishing cry from below, or from inside."*

— *The Devil*

With the devil eliminated it's time to bring *The Resolution* to fruition. No more absolution device, no more blame, no more doubt— no more disconnection.

We begin anew with the dean of human faculties like before, the mind, which is no longer flat. We still don't know everything, but we're ready to allow more possibilities. Our mind still has trouble with dimensions, but we understand realities better with new perspectives. Problems continue to challenge us, but we have the approach and know precisely the plan.

The big brain is not used merely for intimidation anymore, but for delivering us from the human bubble.

Starting with the beginning, which began meticulously deliberate, we subject this new mind. We use it to work out conflicts posed by accidental notions, and recognize Life's unquestionable origin. We recognize that we do not have the copyright to Life. We are thankful to be a part of God's living work.

We no longer reject God, whether by claiming our own originality or by refusing *Their* creations including, but not limited to, humans. We turn our attention to the preparation of God's glorious kingdom. We halt the age-old squandering tradition, build on an endowed beginning, and invest in a better future.

We can read about the past and nourish visions of the future, all the while knowing neither prophets nor prophecies can change God's authorship of Life.

Although "we cannot determine heaven for sure until we get there, we should be very certain of what we expect from its new inhabitants."[1]

We expect to have a relationship with God. Rather than making religion a part-time job or full-time dedication, we trust that God lives within us. Our rhythm reveals our *Parents*, our thoughts reflect *Their* ideals, our actions amplify *Their* original intent— to have an intelligent species spiritually mature on its own.

We expect to make God a dominant lifetime tradition.

We expect the human race to outgrow its spiritual trikes, and achieve complete independence from dogma and other human-made spiritual devices.

Allowing the possibilities of inter-dimensional thoughts, we anticipate a limited-use of our corporal life— yet live permanently without reservation.

---

[1] Taken from *The Heaven.*

Energized by the images of God, we can distinguish between human struggles and God's designs. The power of self-imagery superimposes onto each of our lives the greater image of our *Parents*.

Hope, faith, and the suspicion that God has a plan is overpowered with knowledge. We know there is one absolute Power. We know there is but one Creator, that the universe follows one Governor— that Life obeys one Rule.

We celebrate the knowledge that we, too, belong in Life's formula. We can joyfully accept that we also follow the same Rule. We live to preserve this order without hoping that we can be the exception to it, or having faith that we are favored.

Armed with knowledge, fueled by images of God, freed from the bondage of human struggles, in permanence we charge on.

En garde!

The human resolution, its strategy, and the final approach cannot be stopped— not even by the devil. The once-feared entity is now a moot notion in the human mind.

As a result, humankind will claim victory over life's wretchedness and evil's cruelty.

Assuredly, we will get our *selves* together.

Certainly, we will prevail.

Positively, we know.

We know that heaven is inevitable!

What will Life be like finally in heaven, however heaven is defined or attained?

You have some ideas, and I too have some ideas about what our destination is, how it looks, and how each of our lives will be. I can't help but imagine the luxury, not in terms of material belongings like fast cars and ceaseless money, but of having even a greater power of choice.

Can you imagine? If I do not feel well, I can simply choose to be filled with good health. If I am not happy, I can simply bring myself a festive spirit. You know, if I'm bored with joy, I can easily change my mood into sorrow just for sympathy, then snap out of it at a later time. How about going places, seeing friends, or playing baseball; faster than I can utter any of it, I would be there quickly and simply.

If I could will myself to good health just as I can will myself into sickness, come and think of it— so can you.

Here's the bonus question: How could I bring a smile to your face that you couldn't already bring on your own? Remember, you are also empowered by the essence of heaven. How could I be of assistance to you when you feel down? What thoughts could I share with you if we are already connected?

What can I do for you today?

Actually, nothing.

People, if you want to make a difference, the place is here— and the time is now.

Think about that for a minute.

While you're thinking, imagine an orchestra from a known metropolitan area, where several hundred musicians fill the giant stage in an impressive organization. The instruments dazzle the entire auditorium with brilliant flickers and sparkles from their luster. Imagine that these musicians are each holding the musical instruments for the very first time. Without introduction, they begin to play.

Whew, for crying out loud! All the screeching, scratching, squelching, clinking, thumping, and thrashing amplified by the powerful sound system terrorize our entire bodies. As if to really insult us, we paid in advance. So we sit thinking it's just a silly opening joke. Then we realize that the musicians are sweating heavily, and notice that we, too, are perspiring ourselves. We notice that we are clenching our fists under our laps, grimacing painfully under the dim lights, and slowly losing control due to muscle spasms.

We can tell that the musicians are still trying to produce something, even though nothing, we judge, is about to click any time soon. It's as if they're confident due to a mutual knowledge inside, beyond what we can decipher sitting fast in our seats. It's becoming clearer that we must have fallen asleep and are gnashing our teeth through a musical nightmare. It's for real, unfortunately, and the only thing we are dreaming about is getting our money back. There's probably no chance of that.

As if we suddenly awake from a wide-eyed nightmare, the drummer kicks in, the wind instruments breeze through their pieces, then the strings, and the singers all fall into their musical places.

Without apology— the symphony has begun.

The trumpets revitalize us as the drums keep us true, while the violins console us and the flutes reassure. The piano focuses us, as the organs keep our eyes on the bigger picture.

The cymbals meanwhile proclaim:

It's the Final Victory!

IN FINAL REFLECTION

Now is the time for me to offer you the First Commandment Revisited:

Know your essence— for it's in your Parents' *essence that you are.*
> — *The Resolution*

I am talking about PEACE.
> — *The Devil*

What can I do for you today?
> — *The Final Victory*

If you want to make a difference, the place is here— and the time is now.
> — *Dam-Uyen Tran*

The most incomprehensible thing about the world is that it is comprehensible.
— Albert Einstein

THE MESSIAH

"And Jesus said unto him, Why callest thou me good? There is none good but one, that is, God."

— Mark 10:18, King James Bible

Throughout the centuries, many lives have been brought into the world; some as girls who later blossomed into women, and some as boys who matured into men. They have all come and gone, but none as controversial and paramount as the gentle Nazarene named Jesus.

Not every faith believes in a messiah, and those that do don't always agree on who the Messiah is. While people adamantly proclaim and search for theirs, the world can have but one Messiah.

We cannot refute the possibility that God could send to every faith it's own native-tongue savior. However, if we want to live with that scenario, we must understand that it would require yet another level of tolerance. That is, you would have to accept my Savior while worshipping yours, as they both originate from God.

The time has come for me to dedicate a chapter to those who faithfully follow Jesus, as well as to those who still seek to follow him. I dedicate this chapter to all people who have taken upon themselves to carry a similar cross, and especially to those who try tirelessly to understand the meaning of Jesus' life.

Remember, at all cost and regardless of the individual price, we must assemble one day. This might mean painfully putting aside even the God-given choice to attain the God-authored Truth.

Jesus was not an icon of human religions, but a manifestation of the all-dimensional God.

He was for us, but not by us. He was for us to seek out, learn from, follow along, and know personally. Jesus didn't live in a certain way, because people perceived him that way. He didn't perform certain tasks, because people expected that he would.

While we can only understand him in human terms, our comprehension is required to take flight from ordinary life and language. They're human terms because we are incapable of any other terms. We need to grasp that which we cannot articulate, and comprehend that which we cannot formalize, if we endeavor to understand the Devine.

Ordinary life and language are all that I, too, have to produce this dedication. Never mind the difficulty, in any case, for we should all explore new ways to extend our tools. We will discover that which is beyond the algebraic sums of all our parts, physically as well as mentally.

We must defy the boundaries of traditional language and habitual thoughts, if we are to benefit from this challenging departure.

God saw that the human race needed help in rediscovering themselves, their Creator and *Parents*— so God decided to lend assistance in a direct manner. Regardless of God's approach, *They* had to be consistent in principle and in the message *They* were to convey.

Masterminding this required consistency was critical. God could have simply re-constructed people then. With another blow in the nose, as God created the first human, we would have new memory and self-image. Instead, God opted for the consistent dignified approach. This is the only meaningful approach where people can freely live, think, and decide, using their own faculties.

To ensure this consistency, God must also attain human heights using human apparatus. Otherwise, the intended assistance would be a pointless mockery. People have shown throughout history that they learn best when a teacher can genuinely relate to them, one who can share their strengths and weaknesses. There's no logic in learning to surpass our human tendencies, from a god. It would only serve to underline humankind's inherent weaknesses relative to the Divine.

Foreseeing the implications, God decided to impart *Themselves* to us in full humanness, and completely subjected that part of *Them* to our mortal conditions. Of course, there is little mystery here, as people actually witnessed this imparted member of the greater Body.

This member came to us in the form of a human baby boy. Humankind didn't need to mystify themselves anymore with the esoteric image of their *Parents*. There was an unquestionable image of God living among people now. Though significant, Jesus' origin was not to be as critical as his permanent journey and his destination in Life, ultimately.

Before the meaning of Jesus' journey can enrich us, we must put our previous presumptions aside— here and now. I am not about to take us down the same exploitative path, trodden under by misunderstandings and doubts throughout the past millennia.

It is pivotal that we understand this, or *The Messiah* effectively stops at this point. That is, Jesus turned in his badge and yielded his jurisdiction "upstairs," to seamlessly assimilate with us. Stay with me here. It was as if he changed into coveralls, and left his halo on the nightstand to collect ether dust until his return.

If people should discover that Jesus brought as much as a compact halo with him, all credibility would be in vain. He knew.

He decided to live with his people by the very lessons in Life, which he was about to teach them. He decided to lead humankind genuinely by examples. He decided to sacrifice everything that his children could not grasp to show them, personally, what they can.

He decided to walk through the gate of transformation, the womb of his human mother.

He was God no more!

From this point, we'll address Jesus by name and smaller case *he*, *him*, and *his*. The profound meanings of Jesus' presence in people's lives start from this exact point of understanding onward.

Jesus was God no more.

Jesus was a glaring reminder that people were created in God's image, as Jesus was both by conception, from the work of the Holy Ghost— and by birth, from the delivery into the human race.

"The Holy Spirit was Jesus' father," a confident Christian is quick to argue, "and that's different from us." This is hairsplitting, really, if you think about it. It seems that some people can count their blessings, wait for God's plan, and entrust their lives to God— yet insist that their ability to conceive children doesn't involve the Holy Spirit.

Consistency is necessary, if we are to build entire lives, generations, and traditions around our ideas. Remember, people cannot author Life. We may mate, but it's pompous to suggest that we procreate entirely on our own.

In having Jesus, humankind's origin was irrefutable.

"Jesus didn't come from God," is a common rejection among many non-believers. "He's no messiah." Look, unlike a human king who takes the throne by birth, a messiah garners his kingdom by the impact made on humankind. While people doubt whether Jesus was from God, we need to understand that this issue differs little from the question of whether humans are from God.

Rather than the beginning or the end, the permanent journey is where the Messiah also manifests the definition of his life.

At an early age, Jesus connected with his *Parents* and affirmed his relationship with *Them* by beginning the work he was commissioned to carry out. His daily life was no different from most people of his time. He ate bread and fish, drank water and wine just like everyone else. Unlike human-made deities who inhale foods or don't require any nourishments, Jesus was in every way common and equally perishable.

Realize, too, that the clothing on his back was of the same fabric as the rest of the villagers; the sandals on his feet could have been on yours, if you had the courage to walk in them.

Jesus was baptized with the same water that was used to baptize others. He juggled obedience to his mother, assistance to his father, and his honorable allegiance to God the Most High. He encountered obstacles and faced the same rule of laws of that time. He often spoke about God rather than about kings and rulers of earthly nations. He also assumed and claimed nothing was of his own glory, but attributed all that was good to his *Parents.*

There was one power Jesus seemed to get from his endowment alone— his untainted and unsurpassed trust in God. While people should have envied his uncomplicated relationship with God, it was clear that unsurpassed trust wasn't what many people were looking for at that time.

Understand always, Jesus was endowed with the same faculties, or fundamental abilities, from God just like the rest of the human race. He did not live in a castle, had no bodyguards, and carried no arms. He didn't spend his life erecting steeples or accumulating personal gains, even though he definitely had a following. Not money, might, or influence, but trust alone separated him from his friends and foes.

He was a son, a neighbor, and a mortal man.

However, many people longed for a god in their midst, and subsequently sought to identify, heighten, and glorify the god-ness in Jesus. For thousands of years, people have missed the point entirely.

Many people clouded themselves with failed expectations, thus couldn't benefit from the glorious distinction between the two *man*— Jesus the *man*, and the rest of *man*-kind.

Jesus needed to overcome the obstacles and temptations of the world, and it shouldn't be a surprise that he prevailed.

However, that's where people went tragically wrong several thousand years ago.

We should be very surprised, indeed, for he triumphed with the same devices available to all of us, in areas where people failed.

Jesus didn't wait for subsidies from God. He didn't buckle at his knees, close his eyes, and bow to the underworld. He didn't abandon his responsibility as a contributing member of God's kingdom. He did not ask for wings when no one else had them. He didn't expect God to change the rule of Life for him. He certainly didn't run from his superior lineage of righteousness.

The 2000-year-old wrinkle lies in the fact that humankind was foretold that Jesus was conceived by God, and selfishness blurred our ability to see the man. Additionally, people were preoccupied with personal salvation and miracles— and oblivious to Jesus' glorious distinction.

For example, Jesus fasted for forty days before temptations of the flesh came to him in the mountains. The man was tempted with the very thing he needed to continue living like everyone else and do his work. People saw a man physically, but their motivation saw a god.

What's the meaning of a superman fasting for several weeks, I ask you? Perhaps the 40-day fast was a subtle mockery of the human struggles and their religious rituals.

Did people like to be mocked in Jesus' time?

What about a god baptized by a man?

The man named Jesus had no way of personally turning a stone into bread, any more than anyone else did. You see, if he could have made bread from rocks, his hunger would have been insignificant.

His distinction stood then and stands today, because he did not succumb to fleshy ego. Jesus also didn't dignify his opposition by appealing and enlisting his God.

"When the tempter came, he said, if thou be the Son of God, command that these stones be made bread. But he [Jesus] answered and said, It is written, Man shall not live by bread alone, but by every word that proceedeth out of the mouth of God."[1]

What Jesus demonstrates is that we need not fight back with food, even if food were the temptation. He wisely chose to resist with his strength, instead of foolishly bluffing on his weak stomach. The strength was his intimacy with God, whereas the weakness was the human condition he could not change.

The vast majority of people saw a god triumphed over evil. Come on people, a god versus the devil? So, for the next conservatively two thousand years, people worked diligently to build up some complex mystical values around an event they knew was significant, but didn't comprehend its awesome simplicity.

As books, schools, and religious denominations taught about the incident in the wilderness, the beauty of Jesus became increasingly clouded as people tried to find meaning in it. Now we know what the confusion has been about all this time.

When Jesus suffers in pain, people call him human. When they see miracles, people consider him a god.

People didn't find any miracle in the wilderness that day. Not only did they miss the anticipated spectacle, people began to lose compassion for Jesus, as many of them turned into miracle prospectors. They followed Jesus, as if to map their finds, and were insensitive to another human being fully capable of mortal joy and anguish.

Remember, people already ignored the beauty of a man weakened by a human hunger, who triumphed over himself and temptations of corporal needs.

---

[1] Mathew 4:3-4, *King James Bible.*

Think of the power Jesus must have felt when speaking the plain truth was more convenient. "Man shall not live by bread alone." If we minimize the event by saying, "God triumphed over the devil," then we never saw the parallel between the one *man* and the rest.

Jesus didn't dance around the issue, become rude, or condemn anyone. He didn't even cast blame, pray for intervention, or taunt his status with God.

On occasions, Jesus did things that appeared miraculous. Contrary to long-standing belief, Jesus didn't perform miracles, even though historical writers interpreted the events as miracles. Miracles and magic were no more a part of him than they would ever be of you and me. People expected Jesus to impress them, for they anticipated a god. Jesus insisted repeatedly that he had no special greatness of his own or, at least, not at levels that others couldn't attain.

A blind man praised Jesus after regaining his sight, "And Jesus said unto him, Why callest thou me good? There is none good but one, that is, God."[1]

Jesus was not a deity suppressed in human humbleness, nor was he hiding behind the worldly pretense of humility. He simply *knew* precisely who authored Life, and who was supposed to live it— who is whole, and who are mere fragments.

A man's life had emerged, and a parallel to our own life was drawn. The separation between the two parallels, or lives, rested in the fact that Jesus knew God simply and trusted *Them* perfectly. His pure and permanent relationship with God defined the clear divide along the course of life of the two *man*. While both were humans, one was closer to God. It's like two adjacent paths along a sunset beach, with one path on the closer side to the sun.

---

[1] Mark 10:18, *King James Bible*

Selfishness and temptations constantly coerced the parallel to merge. The resistance to this collapse was the fundamental and surmountable challenge for both *man*. We were supposed to see that only one *man* sustained the forbearance.

More importantly, however— that *man* could.

Understanding this parallel is paramount to our comprehension of a man conceived by God. This understanding is also significant to ultimately knowing our salvation.

Jesus' untainted conviction in God elevated him to the higher latitude, while working from the same endowment. I'm sure it was impossible for people in Jesus' midst to discern which abilities were fortified from his confidence in God, and those common abilities both *man* shared.

People's minds were unwilling to separate Jesus' strengths from his foretold conception. When the water turned to wine, people instinctively connected the wine with the fact that they heard Jesus was God, or from God. This re-association happened seamlessly, and people concluded that because only God has that power, Jesus was God.

The first part of this conclusion is correct, only God has the power to alter reality. The second part of this conclusion shows how desperately people wanted to believe in an abstract divinity, but only in tangible human terms. By persisting that Jesus was God, people also discounted all that God was doing directly for *Their* children. It must have been more convenient connecting the dots between the wine and Jesus in the flesh, than a perceptually distant God.

Jesus worked to demonstrate that perceived miracles and special abilities were not of his own, but of God. There was an imperceptible union between Jesus' knowledge and trust, and God. This close bond with his *Parents* inspired seamless possibilities. Such a communion produced a relationship, or conduit, through which God transformed the water, cured the sick, and repaired the blind, transparently.

A blind man once said to Jesus, "Lord, that I might receive my sight." Jesus said to him, "Go thy way; thy faith hath made thee whole." Immediately thereafter, "he received his sight and followed Jesus in the way."[1]

"Thy faith hath made thee whole." Jesus didn't perform a mysterious operation, prescribe some holy medicine, or pray to God. It wasn't even the words Jesus used. What Jesus said to the man was an observation and an irrefutable fact— not abracadabra.

What appeared to be miracles were God's work conducted through a spiritual conduit between *Parents* and child. Jesus' faith in God was so strong and pure that, at will, he was able to open a precise channel with God. This medium would become conductive, and make possible the transfer of God's work.

Remember, I'm using language in the bubble. "God's work," is the resultant benefit of God's all-pervading, ubiquitous power of Life, and not *Their* selective and deliberate interference, necessarily. It's like resonating with God's rhythm.

The conduit was an integral part of Jesus' life, as he knew with confidence that all of God's children could open it.

It's critical that we understand that Jesus' side of the parallel was identical to the human side, with the difference, of course, in the levels of knowledge and trust in God. Jesus exerted an influence on our path of the parallel swaying it upward to meet with his. Meanwhile, the people's path experienced negative forces, working to keep it from rising to Jesus' side of the divide.

---

[1] Mark 10:51, *King James Bible*

The conflicts and temptations Jesus overcame clearly show that they also tried to erode his relationship with God, as if to gravitate him toward the lower bar of the doubting *man*. The same pressure shackled the lower side, and kept the doubting *man* from rising to Jesus' level.

It was as if to ensure that the two *man* would have to meet, if they could— only at the lower side.

Jesus' forbearance was in his [human] ability to sustain his exemplary life; to show us that we are capable as we're all from the same *Parents*, and to demonstrate the urgent need to close the spiritual gap. His continued maintenance and struggle, against his human tendency to gravitate, was Jesus' most lustrous distinction.

He attained and maintained "human heights using human apparatus."

Many people, on the other hand, were looking for miracles like prospectors panning for gold, and irrecoverably forfeited the living forces of deliverance exemplified by Jesus.

Jesus said, "Follow me!" People knew then as we know now that he wasn't merely talking about dropping our chores, leaving our families, abandoning our responsibilities, and going on tour with him.

He wanted his fellow humankind to pick up their parallel and elevate to his latitude. Instead, most people had casting, fishing, and panning in mind.

Jesus' presence and expounding essence reinforced humankind's innate potentials, reminded us personally of our glorious lineage, and showed us an example of spiritual maturity.

Let us follow him!

Although the parallel of the two *man* never met, it did cross on a rocky path that led to Jesus' crucifixion. On the way to be crucified, many women wept for him, "But Jesus turning unto them said, daughters of Jerusalem, weep not for me, but weep for yourselves, and for your children."[1]

Jesus' death meant that he no longer leads us personally with his exemplary conduct. The upper parallel is no longer visible, and humankind was about to find the beacon, navigate, and distinguish for themselves the genuine path.

Thousands of years later, human lives still don't mirror the one Jesus exemplified. Many people have even lost the vision that Jesus illuminated by the examples of his life. Not only have we not found the upper parallel, tragically, in doubt and distraction, we no longer follow a straight line.

To understand the beauty of Jesus' death, all we need to do is experience it for ourselves. This opportunity was made possible by Jesus, who saw his persecutors with human eyes. He faced them with mortal nerves; he buckled, felled, and died a withering death in the end. We can experience it for ourselves because, like Jesus, we have seen persecution in our lives.

More appalling, perhaps, is that we too have looked into the eyes of the persecuted.

Humankind can feel Jesus' pain as he was overpowered by vicious rage. Jesus made it possible for people to experience both powerful lines of this parallel first hand, so that we may realize the distance still separating us from our *Parents*.

The significance of Jesus' death lies in the fact that we can know that fear was not the only emotion Jesus experienced during his final moments. We know he also suffered cold alienation, clouded bewilderment, as well as vacuous disappointment and terrifying disconnection. Behind those dying

---

[1] Luke 23:28, *King James Bible.*

eyes was humankind's most refined heart in complete mortal loneliness.

How do we know? That's how we, or the remaining *man*, feel when persecuted. Knowing that he was human— we now know how deserted he must have felt.

As one brother knows the quick anger of another, Jesus saw the forsaken intent in his brothers on that incomprehensible day. When he was whipped and tumbled, his heart quivered, for he saw people in relentless rage.

People crucified a brother and friend, and saw him die slowly a human crucifixion. It wasn't human because humans staged it— but because it had to be endured by one.

Unfortunately, many people insist that it was God who died for us on the cross. Many people want the spilled blood to have magic in it. After all, those who killed him did it because "it is written."

It may have been written, but must we punctuate it with a blind eye?

Humankind was foretold that the *man* was coming, but had difficulties identifying the lessons of Life that many people knew were impending. Prospecting for miracles and panning for prophecies, we only look at personal finds, ironically, to forfeit our very fortune.

For the human price Jesus paid, we owe it to ourselves to act swiftly to conquer our hearts and let compassion dominate forever. Oust the flat mind, as we must see the landscape of wisdom.

The *man* didn't succumb to evil forces, but instead illustrated incredible self-control, self-confidence, and self-respect, using only tools that other people possess. The distinction drawn and accented throughout Jesus' life is the sacrifice humankind sorely missed.

The cross is not the only place he shed blood for us. The price is not in the blood on the cross itself, but in the continuance of two similar but distant lives of the two *man*. We must celebrate our capacity to walk the faithful path of the parallel, and ensure that we meet him again in the end.

If we love Jesus, we must know where he bled for us. Was it while dying on the cross— or while seeing us only at a paralleled distance from him?

We must remove our fixation with Jesus' blood. Otherwise, history and lessons are little more than romantic parables. Had he come to us simply to be murdered, we couldn't benefit from his special price.

Our fixation in human's greatest anguish, or death, eclipses us from the trials of Life that Jesus revealed, and the triumph that he invited us to share with him— across the *man-man* divide.

On the third day, he was raised— as Jesus no more.

It's essential to note that Jesus didn't come back from the dead on his own power any more than we could expect you or I to do it. His presence was to glorify his *Parents*. All the glory belonged to God.

Mary Magdalene, a follower who loved Jesus, visited his tomb, "And seeth two angels in white sitting, the one at the head, and the other at the feet, where the body of Jesus had lain."[1]

The angles came to prepare the mortal Jesus for "re-entry." The angles' roles in the resurrection was made overwhelmingly evident when "Jesus saith unto her [Magdalene],

---

[1] John 20:13, *King James Bible.*

'Touch me not; for I am not yet ascended to my Father'."[1] We know he was the human Jesus no more, because Mary talked with him all the while thinking he was a gardener, and did not recognize him.[2]

Jesus wasn't the same. He was no longer the *man* people were supposed to know. As angels delivered Jesus to God, his mission concluded and he returned gloriously as God Himself.

References to *He* now refers to God, specifically, who had once resigned for *man*.

When *He* returns in glory, we must realize that *He* returns as God. Not Jesus, not Messiah, not man!

> *And they found the stone rolled away from the sepulcher [tomb]. And they entered in, and found not the body of the Lord Jesus. And it came to pass, as they were much perplexed thereabout, behold, two men stood by them in shining garments: And as they were afraid, and bowed down their faces to the earth, they [the angels] said unto them, Why seek ye the living among the dead?*
>
> *He is not here....*
>
> – Luke 24:3-6, *King James Bible*

Understand absolutely that the divide was of knowledge and trust of the two *man*. "We can do it!" is clearly written in the median. Humankind can attain spiritual maturity; our lives can mirror Jesus' life long ago; we can reunite with God. A *man* had done it.

Man can achieve the same height again.

Remember, *He* said, "Follow me," or did people hear something else? Jesus wasn't just mocking us, *He* was genuine

---

[1] John 20:16, *King James Bible.*
[2] John 20:15, *King James Bible.*

about people's ability to follow *Him* and pursue the promised kingdom.

We can walk Jesus' path of the parallel!

Proclaim God directly, faithfully, and solely— lest you hypocritically violate the First Commandment you profess is from God. Look again and reconsider, Jesus is no more.

There was, is, and will ever be one God.

One living God!

Teach our children that once upon a time God Almighty became a man, to walk in our sandals but on a higher parallel. *He* has since returned to *His* throne, and it's *man*'s turn to get out of their resignation.

Let's go now, children of all ages, on a perceptual field trip. If we hurry, maybe we'll make it to our destination by noon. Parents and friends come on now, let's all go. We're going to see the Grand Canyon today, okay? Imagine with me as we stand on this side of the barren expanse, we quickly realize that today is an intergalactic field trip day, and everybody is at the canyon.

It's really hot and crowded. Voices from the incredible number of people boom and rumble over the sharp rocks. It's difficult to see around us, but below is a wide open chasm, with but a few big birds rising on the hot air. Be careful, all of you; don't mind the gapping cavity dividing the canyon, just make sure no one takes a deep fall.

Imagine God rips the sky wide open and comes out on the other side. The Grand Canyon suddenly fell silent.

Gradually, we hear horrifying cries from the depths, where birds only earlier soared. No, it's not hell opening from below. No. People are leaping into the canyon thinking that by showing faith in a grand way now, God will deliver them across the great divide, which they have only turned into a spectacle thus far. Meanwhile, others fall to the ground murmuring some familiar chants. We have not seen leaps of faith played out like this, but we've heard these religious murmurs before.

The rest of us stand completely appalled at the disturbing events around us. "Why is all this happening?"

As we look across the vast canyon for clues, it gradually becomes evident that what everybody saw was a reflection on the hazy screen of rising smog.

It's because, for us— God is actually standing on this side.

If only we spend more time looking at one another, we wouldn't see God as distant *Parents*. If only we follow the examples rather than great names and titles, we would be closer to the Truth. If only we stop formalizing, institutionalizing, and complicating the human relationship with God, knowing our *Parents* would come naturally.

If only we insist that "almighty" must mean uniquely one, we could put aside the issue of who is our god, or who is theirs. If only humankind believes in *one* Almighty God, we could embrace one another genuinely and not just politically. We can stop disagreeing, despising, and denouncing ourselves, and live permanently and prosperously in God.

Let us broaden our minds, hearts, and all perceptive faculties, and find intimacy with God, not only through historical testaments, but also through living and changing evidence in humankind. Fossils are instrumental to the understanding of a geological past, but living people are the most convincing confirmation of God's complete glory.

From the beginning of this book, "It is quite clear today that evolutionary scholars, theologians, and common people alike have yet to offer practical answers to the apparent escalating evil around the world." However, things are changing.

In *The Beginning*, we wondered, "Can we prevail?" Now, we understand that it isn't about what we can do, but what we choose to do.

We know.

APPENDIX A

The following original text from the *King James Bible* was used earlier in an interpretation in *The Devil*. Here, it's provided unedited.

Thou sealest up the sum, full of wisdom, and perfect in beauty. Thou hast been in Eden the garden of God; every precious stone was thy covering, the sardius, topaz, and the diamond, the beryl, the onyx, and the jasper, the sapphire, the emerald, and the carbuncle, and gold: the workmanship of thy tabrets and of thy pipes was prepared in thee in the day that thou wast created. Thou art the anointed cherub that covereth; and I have set thee so: thou wast upon the holy mountain of God; thou hast walked up and down in the midst of the stones of fire. Thou wast perfect in thy ways from the day that thou wast created, till iniquity was found in thee. By the multitude of thy merchandise they have filled the midst of thee with violence, and thou hast sinned: therefore I will cast thee as profane out of the mountain of God: and I will destroy thee, O covering cherub, from the midst of the stones of fire. Thine heart was lifted up because of thy beauty, thou hast corrupted thy wisdom by reason of thy brightness: I will cast thee to the ground, I will lay thee before kings, that they may behold thee. Thou hast defiled thy sanctuaries by the multitude of thine iniquities, by the iniquity of thy traffic; therefore will I bring forth a fire from the midst of thee, it shall devour thee, and I will bring thee to ashes upon the earth in the sight of all them that behold thee.

—Ezekiel 28:12-18, King James Bible.

How art thou fallen from heaven, O Lucifer, son of the morning! How art thou cut down to the ground, which didst weaken the nations! For thou hast said in thine heart, I will ascend into heaven, I will exalt my throne above the stars of God: I will sit also upon the mount of the congregation, in the sides of the north: I will ascend above the heights of the clouds; I will be like the most High. Yet thou shalt be brought down to hell, to the sides of the pit. They that see thee shall narrowly look upon thee, and consider thee, saying, Is this the man that made the earth to tremble, that did shake kingdoms; That made the world as a wilderness, and destroyed the cities thereof; that opened not the house of his prisoners? All the kings of the nations, even all of them, lie in glory, every one in his own house. But thou art cast out of thy grave like an abominable branch, and as the raiment of those that are slain, thrust through with a sword, that go down to the stones of the pit; as a carcase trodden under feet.

— Isaiah 14:12-19, King James Bible.

APPENDIX B

Famous quotes personalities

Albert Einstein
(1879-1955)
German-born American Physicist

Aristotle
(384-322BC)
Famous Greek philosopher and scientist

Arnold Glasow
Glasow's Gloombusters by Arnold H. Glasow.

Buddha
(cir. 563bc~483 BC)
Siddhartha Gautama, founder of Buddhism

Chief Seattle
Native American Suquamish Chief

Eleanor Roosevelt
(1884-1962)
Social activist, author, lecturer, and US Representative to the
UN

Empedocles
(Cir. 493~433BC)
Greek philosopher, statesman, and poet

Friedrich Nietzsche
(1844-1900)
German philosopher, poet, and classical philologist

Goethe, Johann Wofgang von
(1749-1832)
German poet, dramatist, novelist, and scientist

Grace Hansen

Mahatma Gandhi
(1869-1948)
Indian nationalist who established freedom without violence

Padmasambha
Famous teacher of Tantric Buddhism during 8th century

Robert M. Pirsig
(cir. 1931-)
Technical writer and former teacher of philosophy
and rhetoric

Socrates
(cir. 470~399 BC)
Greek philosopher

Ursula K. Le Guin
(1929-)
American award winning fantasy, fiction, and children writer.

***

INDEX

***

NOTES

NOTES

NOTES

NOTES